This is a remarkable piece of work. I don't know of any other book that deals with depression and mental illness as powerfully, accessibly and beautifully as Cathy's. It will open your eyes to what it's like to wear a garment of despair when all you want to do is change it for a mantle of praise. For those on the long journey of depression, here is honesty and hope. For those who have depressed friends or family members, here is wisdom - potentially life-changing wisdom. I unreservedly recommend *A Thorn in my Mind*. This book truly connects the reader with Abba, Father's compassionate heart for those whose minds are troubled and whose hearts are broken. You will never be the same after reading it.

Revd Dr Mark Stibbe,
The Father's House Trust

Reading Cathy's story has been a great encouragement and blessing. However, the book is also deeply challenging. Cathy's story challenges me to consider my own perspectives, prejudices and assumptions. It has changed how I understand and have compassion on others. It has changed how I use certain aspects of our English language. And it has totally changed my understanding about those who suffer from mental illnesses. For those who are involved in pastoral ministry, for those who know anyone with a mental illness, for those who know another human being – you should read this book.

Helen Roberts,
Associate Minister,
Watford Community Church

Cathy Wield; A Biography

Cathy Wield was born in India and lived in many different countries while she was growing up. She trained as a doctor, and has worked in Emergency Medicine (A&E) and as a staff grade psychiatrist, in a career that has been interspersed with severe depression.

She is now retired on medical grounds, and lives in Watford, where she continues to write and be actively involved in her local church. Her first book, Life after Darkness, was published in 2006.

She has been married to Phil for over 30 years and has 4 children and 2 grandchildren.

A Thorn in my Mind

Mental Illness, Stigma and the Church

Cathy Wield

instant
apostle

First published in Great Britain in 2012

Instant Apostle
The Hub
3–5 Rickmansworth Road
Watford
Herts
WD18 OGX

British Library Cataloguing-in-Publication Data

A catalogue record for this book is available from the British Library.

This book and all other Instant Apostle books are available from Instant
Apostle:

Website: www.instantapostle.com
E-mail: info@instantapostle.com

ISBN 978-0-9559135-2-5

Printed in Great Britain

Instant Apostle is a new way of getting ideas flowing, between followers of Jesus, and between those who would like to know more about His Kingdom.

It's not just about books and it's not about a one way information flow. It's about building a community where ideas are exchanged. Ideas will be expressed at an appropriate length. Some will take the form of books. But in many cases ideas can be expressed more briefly than in a book. Short books, or pamphlets, will be an important part of what we provide. As with pamphlets of old, these are likely to be opinionated, and produced quickly so that the community can discuss them.

Well known authors are welcome, but we also welcome new writers. We are looking for prophetic voices, authentic and original ideas, produced at any length; quick and relevant, insightful and opinionated. And as the name implies, these will be released very quickly, either as Kindle books or printed texts or both.

Join the community. Get reading, get writing and get discussing!

Table of Contents

Foreword by Dr Rob Waller

Cathy Wield has suffered more than most, with a severe depression starting in her 30s. However she has also seen more of the workings of mental health services than most, both from her work in emergency departments and as a psychiatrist and also from her experience of the treatments offered. These have included medication and psychotherapy, but also electroconvulsive therapy and then neurosurgery.

In all this, she has retained her faith and the belief that God made her just as she is, she has retained her self-esteem as many have accused her for not finding answers within, and she has also retained her desire to help others understand the issues more.

This is not just a biography; it is an informed story, with reflection on the dilemmas it offers. Psychiatry, theology and personal faith lead to compassionate conclusions. A lived experience that will help others live.

Dr Rob Waller,
Consultant Psychiatrist, NHS Lothian,
Director of Mind & Soul

Acknowledgements

I want to thank several people who have read the whole or parts of this manuscript, for their helpful comments and encouragement. They are Helen Roberts, Rob Waller, Keith Matthews, Bob MacVicar, Sunil Raheja and Helen Clark. There are many friends who have prayed for me, supported me and encouraged me and to them I give my sincere thanks.

I am grateful to Noel Richards for his permission to use his song, and to Jonathan Clark for permission to use part of his talk that he gave at a Mind & Soul conference.

I am also very grateful to Becky Fawcett of Authentic Media for her help and input.

Finally I would like to pay tribute to my husband Phil, without whom I could not have embarked on the writing of this book. He has been a tireless source of wisdom and encouragement. I must also thank my family for supporting me through this time.

I have enjoyed working with Bridget Adams and Manoj Raithatha of Instant Apostle Ltd and am very grateful to be published during their launch of this exciting new company.

Introduction

I have a passion for the mentally ill. I want to see stigma eliminated, to see change, to witness God working in lives which have otherwise been blighted and I long to see the Church taking the lead on this as she often has done in the past; justice needs to be done for those with mental illness, in the way they are treated within churches, within the health services as well as within society in general and no sufferer should be without hope. This is why I am writing primarily but not exclusively for Christians. I am a doctor, but also a patient and have experienced many of the treatments which are available for those who are mentally ill, including ECT and even brain surgery. Yet I am a normal woman, still married, with four grown up children and part of a thriving church. As I journey for the rest of my life, I never want to stop doing the things God wants me to do, despite my illness, going where He wants me to go and growing more like Him. What a challenge, but God is in control and my trust must always be in Him, my Father, Jesus and the Holy Spirit.

Isaiah's Call

The Spirit of the Sovereign Lord is on me, because the Lord has anointed me to preach good news to the poor. He has sent me to bind up the broken-hearted, to proclaim freedom for the captives and release from darkness for the prisoners, to proclaim the year of the Lord's favour and the day of vengeance of our God, to comfort all who mourn, and provide for those who grieve in Zion – to bestow on them a crown of beauty instead of ashes, the oil of gladness instead of mourning, and a garment of praise instead of a spirit of despair. They will be called oaks of righteousness, a planting of the Lord for the display of his splendour. Isaiah 61:1–3

This passage is utterly inspirational, fulfilled by the coming of Jesus (Luke 4:18–21) and a prophetic mandate to release those who are held captive by darkness in one form or another. I have been broken-hearted, a captive, a prisoner to mental illness in the form of depression. I have mourned as one who has lost and I have grieved yet all the while being a Christian – one who is 'in Zion', but I have also been given a crown of beauty, the oil of gladness and a garment of praise.

Even more exciting as the passage goes on, it says that those who have been released will become the new builders who will 'restore the places long devastated' and 'they will renew the ruined cities'. So I see the future for those who have long been held captive to mental illness as much as captive to anything else.

This is not only an account of my personal release, but it is also a handbook for everyone who is in contact with those who are prisoners to mental illness, even if only for a short while, be they in your family, your workplace, your community or in your church.

Although I am a woman speaking of mental health issues, this message is not just for women. Men are also affected by mental illness, though it may well be more hidden. The stigma of mental ill health is still present within our society and churches, but maybe more so for men than even for women. However, let me never forget that our Lord discriminates against no one, but He wishes for all mankind to be saved and all of us to be free of whatever hinders our relationship with Him and with His will for our lives.

4

While I suffered severe depression, advice came at me from all sides. If it wasn't the neighbour down the road suggesting cranial acupuncture, it was my Christian friend telling me of a book or a ministry that had helped them. There are many, many books on the shelves purporting to have the answer. This is not one of them. I merely share my life with you and want to give hope to those who are afflicted in this way, that God has not left them, far be it, He has purpose for their lives even when everything around is saying the complete opposite.

Paul's Thorn in the Flesh

Therefore, in order to keep me from becoming conceited, I was given a thorn in my flesh, a messenger of Satan, to torment me. Three times I pleaded with the Lord to take it away from me. But he said to me, 'My grace is sufficient for you, for my power is made perfect in weakness.' Therefore I will boast all the more gladly about my weaknesses, so that Christ's power may rest on me. 2 Corinthians 12:9

As I read these words written by the apostle Paul, my heart is warmed. We don't know what Paul's thorn in the flesh was, though many have speculated, but it is God's response to his pleading to have it removed that is so heartening. God's grace, His undeserved favour, is always enough and just in case we think we are still not up for the job, we are reminded that God's power is made perfect in our weakness. We can't lose!

My 'thorn' took me by surprise when I was 34 years old. It seemed to have come out of the blue, for me it consisted of my first episode of severe depression which went on to last for a period of seven long years. During that time, I did plead with the Lord to take it away many times, but I did not seem to hear a response. Yet all through that time, I never doubted that

God was there. Strangely I was not angry at God either and on the two occasions when I made attempts on my life, I fully believed that through Jesus' death on the cross, I was forgiven and therefore was on my way to heaven.

Thankfully the Lord had other ideas for my life and He kept me safe to experience a miraculous recovery. But I would not have found myself describing this depression as a 'thorn in my mind' until a few years after my recovery from that first episode. It is only now when, most of the time, I enjoy good health, that I realise I have to live with the consequences of this illness and I can, like Paul, boast of my weaknesses because God is good. He has done so much for me as I make this incredible journey that is my life.

I am a qualified doctor and most of my working life has been spent training in Emergency Medicine, or A&E. However I have also worked as a staff grade psychiatrist, so I have a fair bit of experience on both the giving and the receiving end of the NHS. But if I had known when I was a fresh, young medical student that I would be writing about mental illness, *my mental illness*, I would have been devastated. I held the attitude that it was only weak people who suffered from such disorders and that more often than not they could be the cure for themselves. I had heard of people having breakdowns, and had observed my mother's anguish when she received the news of someone she knew becoming unwell in this way. But it was definitely something that happened to other people, certainly not to me or my family. I was not aware of my vulnerabilities as I went through boarding school, but in any case that was a thing of the past. I came from a strong, confident family who found it easy to be opinionated. Though I was hard working and ambitious my mother has always described me as sensitive. I remember when I was aged nine and *Oliver* had come out at the cinema, she wouldn't let me go and see it, because I had had nightmares after seeing *Chitty, Chitty, Bang, Bang!*

Victory in Christ

My experience has made me realise that my outlook towards the mentally ill was rather arrogant, but in my defence, I really hadn't come face to face with anyone I knew to be suffering from it. That in itself was rather amazing, but I know it wasn't talked about much even though the truth is that certainly as adults, mental illness affects all of us directly or indirectly. An episode of mental ill-health will be suffered by 1 in 4 of us at some time in our lives and now it has come into the open, we will almost certainly come across those who are held in its grip, whether it is through personal experience or that of friends or family.

However as Christians we are on the winning side; we have the victory in Jesus' name, praise God and we are loved. 'For I am convinced that neither death, nor life, nor angels, nor principalities, nor things present, not things to come, nor powers, not height, nor depth, nor any other created thing, will be able to separate us from the love of God, which is in Christ Jesus our Lord.' (Romans 8:38–39) What a wonderful piece of scripture and how true it is and has been throughout my somewhat turbulent life! God is good; He always has been and always will be. He is amazing and even when subject to an illness like depression as I have been, there is always hope. Not just hope for the future, or even hope for healing, but hope of a life more and more dependent on Him; He can bring laughter and joy into our lives, because of what Jesus has done for us. I do not underestimate the gravity of some mental illness but, even in serious cases, He can use us to release the captives and set the prisoners free.

It is not always easy to deal with someone who has mental illness; I couldn't deal with 'me' when I was ill, so how could I expect anyone else to? When I had come across the mentally ill as an adult the very idea invariably provoked feelings of fear in me. How will 'they' behave, what will I say, what can I do, will I be able to cope? I was afraid that I might say the wrong thing and yes, I did from time to time, specifically when a close friend of mine was ill at medical school. But now I hope I have a greater understanding of mental illness and want to share this with fellow Christians, so that our collective heart's desire, which is to be compassionate and sympathetic, may be realised.

I wonder what came to mind when I as a church member thought of the mentally ill. What I think has certainly changed since I have experienced it myself. Before then, I used to stereotype the mentally ill – they would be wearing drab clothing, unable to look anyone in the eye, distinctly peculiar and not people you would want to be with. I am not proud to admit that. Yet mental illness is common and actually sufferers are normal people like you and me and they will be found at school, at college, at work, in the community and therefore in the church. None of us are immune. Given the right set of circumstances, we could all have a run in with some of the disorders which come under the banner of mental illness. Of course it is not catching, yet the world often isolates the mentally ill as though we are infected, so as a consequence we hide our disease. It's time for us to speak out, it's time to show that it is not necessarily a lifelong affliction and even when it is, nothing can separate us from the love of God and all that He has for us.

Mental illness is a universal problem and does consist of many separate disorders, but there seems to be an epidemic going on in the Western world. I am writing not just about my own experience of mental illness, but also about related topics important to us who are of the Christian tradition and give information about the various mental illnesses that occur and the treatments available for them.

The Stigma of Mental Illness

There is also the phenomenon of stigma associated with mental illness, which is rife in society in the UK, but much more so in some other cultures and nations throughout the world. In our own country, there have been nationwide campaigns here to change how we think about mental illness – eg the 'Defeat Depression Campaign' and more recently 'Time to change. Let's end mental health discrimination'. They have made a difference but not as much as was hoped.

I attended a conference on 'Christians the Bible and Psychology' in London in 2010. The question was put to the floor as to whether there was more stigma within the churches or outside in the world and sadly an overwhelming majority voted 'within the churches'. In disgrace, I have to admit that I have demonstrated stigma in my own attitude before I suffered myself, not just as a Christian but as a doctor as well. I am truly ashamed of that now and yet at the time, I did not see myself as being wrong or hypocritical. Rather it was a comfort to retreat into the collective view that those who feel insecure about the whole business of mental illness have; as the medics would say the sad, the mad and the bad. I have had to repent of my attitude once I saw it for what it was, but I fully understand how anyone can hold these other views. However I hope and pray that it won't be for long.

The Oxford English Dictionary describes stigma as 'a mark or sign of disgrace or discredit'. In this instance I want to refer to it in regard to mental illness or mental health problems, but I hope it will be clear that some of the principles can also apply to other situations where people feel a bit as though they are outcasts. I heard a presenter on Radio 4 talking about the new definitions of mental illness, which will be classified by the American DSM (diagnostic and statistical manual); he was expressing doubts as to whether the categories have become too broad and would therefore put more people under the *stigma* of having a mental illness. That's an admission in itself – stigma is what society expects, but now is the time to change. The causes are multiple and are often to do with ignorance and a lack of knowledge or understanding; this can be corrected by education, but another cause of stigma is fear. There is fear of the unknown, but also fear of *what is known*. This can be illustrated with a brief history of mental illness, or 'madness' as it was called back in our past – this will be described in one of the chapters.

The media can be helpful in promoting the news and views of celebrities and authors who have suffered from mental health problems, but, unfortunately, they are also responsible for some of the misconceptions that easily arise. For instance, most murders are carried out by someone known to the victim, usually a family member, but this will not be reported on. Yet I cringe when mental illness is mentioned if the perpetrator happens to be being treated, despite the fact that the vast majority of patients with mental illness are not in the least bit violent. A lot of murder mystery dramas portray the murderer as being mentally ill, with similar consequences, and when the rare occurrence happens that a mentally ill person does carry out an attack on a member of the public, the press are all too ready not only to report it, but to raise questions as to whether or not that person should have been compulsorily detained to prevent the crime. Unfortunately this sends out the message that those with mental illness are dangerous and should be locked up, when in fact this is rarely the case. Those friends and relatives who end up killing someone close to them can't be locked up before a crime is committed, yet murder in those circumstances is very much more common.

Cases of suicide which involve other people, like the murder of a child committed by the suicidal parent, or a train crash which inevitably involves the driver, are also reported with vivid descriptions and if possible photographic evidence.

10

Again this is not common, but the desperate agony of the suicide victim is rarely discussed; for most suicides, if they are reported at all, it is the pain of the friends and family which are described. The absolute loneliness and despair that drives people to end their own lives is not often talked about, nor is the fact that, for most victims, correct and sufficient psychiatric treatment might well have saved them. But I have to distance myself from the ritual suicides which have taken place in some cults and indeed from the destructive behaviour of the suicide bombers which have brought such awful devastation in many parts of the world – we certainly seem to hear more about them.

I do believe that we as Christians can reverse the stigma of mental illness within the Church and I hope that we can lead the way in accepting and supporting any vulnerable person, affected by mental health issues or not, whether as a temporary affliction or a more permanent disability.

I was a Christian when I fell ill and a church member and I lost my way for a short time but through my illness I have grown up in many ways. During my journey I learned more about what it is to be a child of God and that He is not just my saviour, but my Father, my *Abba*, my Dad as well. I had a diagnosis of severe intractable depression. That was bad enough, now I have a diagnosis of recurrent severe depression. That has taken more getting used to, so I speak out of personal experience. I continue on my journey wondering what else God has in store for me and know that despite my difficulties, He never gives up, so I must not do so either.

Here is a quote from James Olthius, a Professor of Theology and a psychotherapist, which I find really helpful and wish I had known about it sooner.

Judging from the number of people who have come into my office admitting that they would have come for help sooner if they hadn't felt pressured to pretend to be happy, every church, synagogue, or mosque should have a flashing neon sign: SEVERELY DEPRESSED PEOPLE MAY HAVE A STRONG AND SURE FAITH. Many people suffering from depression are haunted by guilt and a quiet desperation that their faith is inauthentic. They are convinced that if their faith were real, they would be filled with joy; because they are not filled with joy, their faith must be counterfeit. For such people, it can be a tremendous relief to realize that their faith commitment can be genuine even if they are incapable of feeling it at this time or in this space. This realization can open up the emotional space necessary for dealing with the depression. (The Beautiful Risk, Grand Rapids: Zondervan, 2001)

It is so simple, yet deeply profound and I would have liked to circulate it throughout the church before I suffered my illness, as I identify so much with what he describes. My hope is that readers will catch 'the vision' and experience more understanding about some of the mental illnesses as well as what it is like to suffer from one as I have, albeit to an extreme degree.

1: The Joy of the Lord

As a Christian I am supposed to be one of the most joyous people on all the earth; the Old Testament tells us to sing for joy (Psalm 81:1), to shout to the Lord with joy (Psalm 47:1) and that the joy of the Lord is our strength (Nehemiah 8:10). In the New Testament, there are numerous references – that joy may be in us (John 15:11), 'the disciples were filled with joy and the Holy Spirit' (Acts 13:52) and 'consider it pure joy...whenever you face trials' (James 1:2) but I have not always been in the reality of this. I am not always filled with joy. I do not always find that the joy of the Lord is my strength because for much of the time, I operate in my own strength and when that runs out I can't always harness the joy. I do not believe that I am alone in my experience and although this is a fruit of the Spirit (Galatians 5:22), there are too many occasions where the Spirit is not getting a look in!

Unhappiness in Christian circles comes in many guises; the religious Christian who lives their life according to rules and regulations, the lonely Christian who cannot find friendship and fellowship which they are desperately longing for, the bitter Christian who has not yet learned to forgive as 'we have been forgiven', the bereaved Christian who has lost someone or something dear to them and the sick Christian weighed down by the burdens of ill health, to name but a few. I think at one time of my life or other, I could have fitted any of those descriptions and in the midst of this unhappiness, I admit to spending a number of years being anything but joyful when I was struck down with depression. The term depression is well known, but actually it is certainly not a single entity. It means different things to different people, varying from an expression of mild sadness to a serious illness which threatens a sufferer's very existence. The first episode I went through was so awful and the subsequent problems I have had have not been anything like as severe or as prolonged, so once again I am able to experience a deep joy! But something I heard alarms me. Apparently some would have it that if you are really a Christian, you cannot be depressed. Is this true? I know it isn't, there is plenty of evidence of biblical characters being depressed, but such questions disturb me as I don't want to defend myself, especially when I am feeling in the depths of despair.

Sadly I have not made it easy for myself to show what is really going on in my life. I have used many cover ups; an identity to suit the occasion. It is not always easy to reveal the 'real me' to myself, let alone to other people. The Sunday church service or meeting, just like at a social occasion or in my job as a hospital doctor, may involve just as much play acting as if I was one of those hopefuls auditioning for a part in the local pantomime.

Where has reality gone? Did it ever exist? Why am I so reluctant to open myself up to other people? Why do I not want to go deeper? Yes, I am asking myself these questions.

I am not suggesting that I become insensitive and hurtful, brutal honesty is not what I am after. Nor, am I suggesting that I answer every enquiry about my health with a long list of my current woes. But quietly, without being shocked at one another, I need to get off the path of looking good for my own benefit and start facing my brokenness, my longing to get right, my longing to become more like Jesus. I need to admit that I am a frail human being, imperfect, overly proud, but on a great journey with God to a fantastic homecoming in eternity. In doing so, I believe that I have opened the flood gates to expressing joy as well as sadness, which is almost certainly buried somewhere within my suppressed emotions.

Some Family Background

I was not raised in a Christian family. My parents were adamant that their four children might be free to choose any religion they wanted to follow, or not as the case may be. They did *not* have us christened (infant baptism) in accordance with this and their own beliefs, which in their day was much more unusual than it is today.

My father was a diplomat and posted overseas for the majority of my childhood. I was born in India and spent my first year under the watchful eye of a nanny. Four years of my primary education took place in a convent school in Nairobi, Kenya and from there we moved to Bangkok in Thailand. In the convent I was introduced to God, but not perhaps in a way that I could say steered my spiritual growth. I came home from school one day and announced to my mother, 'I saw God today. They keep Him in a box!' Apparently I had been shown a religious relic! Then there was some confusion as I was being prepared for first communion, which I described as 'going to have tea with Jesus', before it was established that in fact I was not a Catholic and I was quickly reassigned to the protestant class.

After nine months at an English school in Bangkok, my parents returned to the UK and this was the time when I was started at boarding at Badminton School in Bristol, a month before my tenth birthday.

This seemed to be the start of my troubles. I really thought I wanted to go to boarding school until I actually got there. That first night, I cried myself to sleep. Suddenly I felt very much alone and wished I was back at home. I settled in to some extent, but unfortunately it took me a long time to get over my homesickness. In fact life took on a cyclical nature. All term, I longed for the holidays (by this time my parents and two younger sisters had returned to Thailand), and all holidays I dreaded going back to school.

I had another cause for my unhappiness though. At eight years old, I told a big lie to my parents. It started innocently enough. We were in England for a few months before we went to Thailand. At the local primary school the head teacher had warned us during one assembly about threats to school children. I had a very vivid imagination and for no apparent reason, I went home and told my mother that I had been threatened on the way to school. I had no anticipation of what this lie could mean. The next thing I knew was the police came round to find out what had happened – I couldn't pull out then and so started a local search for a man that never existed.

That same night came the realisation that I was a bad person. I remembered how I had taken money from the change my father used to leave on the dressing table. Guilt started in earnest, yet it was not followed by any confessions to my parents. I was too scared of being rejected if they knew what a bad person I was. The guilt plagued me and it came with me to boarding school.

I told one of my friends about my guilt and she must have told her mother because I received a letter from her telling me about Jesus; but I couldn't understand what she was trying to convey to me and that seemed to be the end of that. Now, I am sure Elizabeth's mother must have been praying for me and I wish she knew her prayers were answered!

A few years later, because I was still having trouble with homesickness, my parents decided that I should be moved to a more 'homely' school. In fact, it made things ten times worse as, just before I changed school, I suddenly started to thrive at Badminton. Yet God's hand was in it.

The new school was close to London, where my uncle Douglas McBain and his family lived. I was to go there for my exeats and half terms while my parents were still in Thailand.

On the first weekend I spent with them, I learned what it meant that my uncle was a Baptist minister. To my chagrin, I had to go to church with them. Amazingly for me, Douglas preached a message of salvation that Sunday morning. I was by this time 14 years old – in his sermon he said that this Jesus forgives our sins, removing our guilt and shame. I had never heard that before, so I eagerly asked Jesus into my life and came out of church feeling a different person; I felt lighter and free as the guilt that plagued my life had disappeared and I was grinning from ear to ear. My cousin Alison, who was to become a lifelong friend, asked me if anything had happened. I said 'no' as I had no real idea as to what had taken place, but I did express the desire to be christened! They then ascertained that I had made the most important decision of my life. I had become a Christian and within a few weeks, my uncle baptised me by full immersion in his church, Lewin Road Baptist Church, in Streatham, South London. I heard about the Holy Spirit very soon after giving my life to Jesus and not long afterwards I was baptised in the Holy Spirit and was given the gift of tongues. I was young and knew nothing of the scriptures or indeed any church related controversies. I was eager to learn and to be baptised in the Holy Spirit, as well as being scriptural, was completely natural to me (see Mark 1:8).

From then on, I loved staying with the McBains and my aunt, uncle and cousins became a second family to me. I spent as much time there as I could when allowed out of school.

Moving on

Returning to school after that weekend away, I was more than a little shocked at the reactions of my classmates, after my dramatic conversion. I couldn't wait to tell them, but my enthusiasm was greeted with disdain. They said that they were Christians already as they went to church and had been christened as infants. My story meant little to most of them, but my friend Mandi told me years later that she did actually become a Christian when I prayed the prayer of salvation with her, though there didn't seem to be any meaningful response at the time. My school was a Church of England school, but the head teacher did her best to allow me to integrate my new found faith, allowing me to attend a local Baptist church; inevitably though, a teenager in school uniform, being brought by taxi for the Sunday morning service did not find me the necessary friendships with the local young people. Although a family from the church did take an interest in me, it was not enough and I stopped going. I have absolutely nothing against Anglican churches, but, though I went with the school, our local church was not lively.

My parents had moved to Chiang Mai, in the north of Thailand where my father was the British Consul. It was a small town, set on the banks of the river Ping; it was easy to go out to the hills which were covered in tropical forest and the climate was much more conducive than the heat and humidity of Bangkok where we had been living. During school holidays when I flew back home, I loved wandering around the town with my mother, visiting the little shops, amongst other things looking out for original Ming china amongst the many replicas which were being sold. I also met other Christians because, at that time, a lot of the Westerners located there were missionaries. When I made it known that I wanted to become a doctor, I was invited to go and watch some operations at the Leprosy Mission Hospital. I determined that I would like to become a surgeon too, so, back at school, I concentrated on my studies. Whilst in Chiang Mai I attended church and joined in with the local prayer meetings. My parents did not stop me going although I knew they silently disapproved. They had been subjected to harassment at cocktail parties when some overzealous missionaries had shown their own objection to alcohol consumption by parking their cars outside and playing Christian music very loudly. This did not endear my parents to my newfound faith.

The posting to Thailand came to an end and my parents returned to England so both my contact with my uncle's family and the missionaries stopped. Unfortunately I stagnated spiritually as I had no further contact with Christians.

However another remarkable thing happened. I retained my desire to become a doctor and was offered a place at St George's Medical School in Tooting. I hadn't looked at the geography of the area and so when I arrived to start at medical school, I was surprised and delighted to find some students of the Christian Union were waiting for me. Some of them were attending Lewin Road Baptist church – I was not five miles away from Streatham, my uncle and his family.

I took up where I had left off both with my spiritual life and also with the friendship of my cousin Alison and started attending 'Lewin' regularly.

I loved being at medical school and threw myself into various activities and enjoyed having lots of new friends. But once I was in the second year, I found that one thing did bother me particularly and that was the fact that I didn't have a boyfriend. I was sweet 19 and had never been kissed! I went to see one of the church elders, a wise, old man by the name of Albert. What he said was definitely what I did not want to hear. He told me that I didn't need a boyfriend, but that the Lord was preparing me to meet my husband. But I was only in my second year at medical school and I didn't want to get married for years, so I went back to the halls of residence feeling even more disgruntled.

My parents had returned abroad again, this time to Brunei, but the foreign office only paid for one airfare a year now I was a student; I decided to spend my long summer vacation of my second year in England, planning to visit Brunei at Christmas instead. For the holiday I worked as a mortuary assistant and also did some night shifts as a nursing auxiliary. Most of my friends were home, so I was a bit lonely and on one particular Sunday in August, I jumped at the chance to go out to a concert with a group of clinical students from church (who did not get the long holiday). I walked with a friend of theirs called Phil. He was not a medical student, but had recently got a job as a computer programmer for the NHS. My prayer for a boyfriend was being answered, I fancied him and to my surprise he seemed to like me too.

We started going out together and I couldn't wait to see him after a day at work. After three weeks, we were at East Croydon station waiting to get a train when, out of the blue, he asked me to marry him! This was totally unexpected as was my answer of 'yes'. I remember surprising myself. I hadn't prayed about this or put it before God and I had just agreed to a lifelong commitment! I prayed after the event though, and remembered Albert's words to me; fortunately, despite some initial turmoil, I was excited and believed that I had made the right decision to spend the rest of my life with Phil. We were madly in love, but decided we wouldn't tell anyone until Phil had gone out to meet my parents in Brunei at Christmas.

Phil had long hair and a beard, which I knew would cause my parents some concern, so he had them cut short before making his journey. We waited until New Year's Eve before we announced our engagement, but my parents weren't altogether happy. Who was this man to interrupt my important studies to become a doctor? However after a reassuring letter from Phil confirming his commitment to support me, they turned around, accepted our decision and we made plans for the wedding to take place in the following August, when they would be home on leave. Uncle Douglas was delighted to marry us and we took on the new role of being a couple in the church. However I had not lost my aspiration to become a surgeon. Maybe one day we would become missionaries ourselves but for now I had to concentrate on my studies.

All Things New

Since being married, I had another battle going on in my personal life. I became broody, not helped by becoming friends with other young couples in the church who had new babies. I talked over my feelings with Phil and we both came to the conclusion that now was not the right time to start a family and, furthermore, if for some reason I fell pregnant, I would have to give up medical school and that was not what we were prepared to do. We decided that we still had a few years to wait before we could think of settling down and starting a family

About a year later, I started to feel queasy. I remarked to my house group leader Penny, who was a Mum herself, that I had gone off coffee and she helpfully asked me whether I was pregnant. I denied this, but kept the conversation to myself. Although convinced that I wasn't pregnant, doubt had been seeded in my mind and the following day I decided to take a pregnancy test just to make sure. In those days, the test was done at a chemist shop and, while I was waiting for the results, I went out and bought a tight dress as if to reassure myself.

I was shocked at the result – positive! I only had 18 months to go at medical school until I qualified; I couldn't give up now. I was terrified. Initially I had little thought of God in this except to know that under no circumstances would I end the pregnancy. I was crying my eyes out at the dilemma when I phoned Phil from the call box, but, to my delight, he came home early with flowers in his hand and he agreed with me that I should not give up my studies. We committed our new circumstances into the Lord's hands.

The medical school were not unduly concerned that I was pregnant; the only change that was made to my study programme was that my final surgical placement, which would take place in the last two months of my pregnancy, would be in the same hospital where I was due to give birth.

I was on the last day of this placement when I went into labour whilst assisting the surgeon with an operation. I told no one, but quietly timed the contractions on the theatre clock. After that I went straight over to the labour ward to meet my midwife! It was early Friday afternoon and around 6am the following morning Rebecca Faith was born. We were thrilled and delighted. I felt so fulfilled now I was a mother. God was praised!

A strange thing happened though; almost immediately after the birth, I lost my aspiration to be a surgeon. Now my only desire was to be at home with my baby but I had just entered my final year, so I knew I needed to finish medical school. It was a really hard dilemma to face. Beforehand I had felt

so comfortable to know that my baby would be looked after by someone else, now more than anything I just wanted to be with her.

God's hand continued to be with us. The Monday following Rebecca's birth was the beginning of two weeks study leave before four written finals, and somehow I did try and revise as best I could with our new baby. Phil sat with her in the car as I did the exams and I came out to our little daughter who was by then desperate for another feed.

However when the results came, they were disappointing. I had only managed to pass two out of the four exams. I went to see the Dean of the medical school. She happened to be a paediatrician and was very sympathetic to my case. My next placement was the elective, during which most students go to spend time at hospitals overseas. I had arranged a more local position, but the Dean told me that I was to have the three months as study leave to retake the exams and to look after my baby. She assured me that my experience of motherhood would stand me in very good stead as a doctor! The Lord had it all under control.

By then, we were meeting with a few other couples to start a new church under the covering of Southampton Community Church, part of the so called 'House Church Movement'. We moved into the home of one of these couples when the house that we lived in was unbearably cold that winter. We had no heating apart from a gas fire in the living room; there was an outside loo and a bath in the kitchen. Andy and Rebecca had also had a baby a couple of months before us and Rebecca had kindly offered to look after our baby, Becs, for the few months I had left at medical school until the completion of the rest of my final exams. It was indeed God's grace to us that I managed to pass them all this time. At last I had made it, I was a qualified doctor! However, after qualifying, a young doctor had to do house jobs, (now known as the pre-registration or foundation year) but in those days it was expected that you work an 80–120 hour week and there was no option to do this part time. I did not want to work like that for the next year with such a young child, so instead I became an enthusiastic full time mum.

We were very committed to our little church and we were learning much about the Bible and spiritual growth at that time. God continued to bless us; just before qualifying, we had moved into a flat that we had managed to buy with a 100% mortgage. It needed complete renovation as it was in a terrible state, but we were so pleased with the purchase. To help finance this, we decided to rent a room out to a lodger. A lovely nurse called Cara moved in who was also part of our little church. I was so happy when I became pregnant for a second time.

I was very content with being a mother despite the fact that Becs had suffered from bad eczema, for which I was advised to exclusively breast feed her until six months of age. Then, as she grew older, she started wheezing and we had many admissions to hospital as she developed asthma. Fortunately Simon and then Stephanie, our third child, did not have such allergy problems.

When Stephanie was a baby, we started thinking about going abroad to work and we felt that the Lord was speaking to us about Asia. Phil made enquiries about getting a computer job, but none of these led anywhere.

One morning, a newsletter came from a charity called Christian Outreach – Cara, our former lodger, had gone to work with them out in Thailand. I noticed that the position of Country Director was vacant. I don't know what gave me the confidence to phone them and offer Phil as a potential candidate. I knew he wouldn't do this himself as he would exclude himself as being completely unqualified for the job, which in reality was true. However when I admitted to him just what I had done, I was expecting a deserved reprimand, but instead he felt a strange peace. The organisation (now known as CORD), had not taken on married personnel let alone whole families as volunteers, but as they got to know us, it became clear that we were the right people for the work. So in April 1987 when Rebecca was 4, Simon 2 and Stephanie just 1 year old, we embarked on a new adventure as Phil took up the post of Director (Thailand) for Christian Outreach. We lived in Bangkok but most of the team worked in the heavily guarded camps which housed the Cambodian displaced peoples on the Thai-Kampuchean border. I was so pleased to return to Thailand and to relearn the Thai that I had picked up in my childhood.

The housing market had favoured us in London. We had been able to sell our flat at considerable profit and buy a house, which we also did up. Now we needed to sell it and had decided that on our return to the UK after two years, we would settle in Southampton. My parents by this time had retired and were helping us to buy a property after the sale of the London house finally went through. Unfortunately by the time they had got hold of us by phone and described the house they had viewed, the buoyant market had snapped it up. Gazumping was commonplace.

We agreed that I should fly back to England and try to buy a house in Southampton myself. A couple of days before I was due to leave, we realised that the children were on my visa for Thailand. I could not leave the country without them, so I arrived in Southampton with the three young children in tow! Again God was so good to us. Somehow, I managed to see a suitable house, buy it, move our furniture in, find tenants and rent it out all within three weeks! I phoned Phil to say the job was done, but also to inform him that I was feeling sick as was usual when I fell pregnant. Our fourth baby was on the way!

Phil had really taken to the job in Thailand and far preferred this new line of work to the IT jobs he had left behind, but after two years we believed that we needed to get the older two children into school and to start earning a living again. Before we left Thailand in 1989, a member of the Christian Outreach team decided to video a typical day in my life. I look back in wonder as I home schooled Rebecca surrounded by Simon and Stephanie joining in with active play and our new baby Jonathan on my lap!

We immediately felt at home when we joined the church back in Southampton and with our growing family soon made friends, particularly with those who had young children like ourselves. Phil had wanted to continue in charity work on our return, but the UK charities were not interested in his experience because it took place overseas. So once again he took a job with an IT company as a systems analyst and programmer.

Starting Life as a Doctor

I remained convinced that my role as a wife and mother was very important in the Lord's eyes, even though more and more women were going out to work, and I continued to be more than content. However Phil was finding his work extremely tedious and I was aware that should I need to work as a doctor in the future, I would need to do my pre-registration house jobs. I felt guilty that I was letting my principles down; I believed I should be there for my children. But when we talked it over, a solution emerged. Phil would look after the children while I returned to medicine.

Another miracle happened, after eight years away from medicine since qualifying, I was offered a job as a house surgeon in Basingstoke. Phil's company went bankrupt just after he resigned and the role swap was under way. Of course I missed my former occupation as housewife, but I threw myself into the job as junior doctor and soon six months had passed. Phil meantime had paid scant attention to the 'how to do it' book I had written for him and loved his role as househusband! For the next year we were to share our duties, as I was able to do the other part of my house jobs as a job share with another young mother. We worked one week on, one week off and our idea had been that on my week off, Phil would pick up computer work so that the bills could be paid. However our plan wasn't going too well. Phil wasn't getting much work, so I started working locums when I was off and Phil continued to spend the majority of his time looking after our children, three of whom were by now at school.

Finally we decided that I should do the three year training to become a GP full time, in our complete role swap. I enjoyed medicine but loved my time off at home with the children. Our family continued to take precedence in our lives.

I had two six month posts in A&E (Accident and Emergency) as an SHO (senior house officer) in Southampton and during the second post met a new consultant by the name of Lynn Williams. I preferred the speciality to the six month post I had spent in General Practice, but I was increasingly feeling the strain of working full time in medicine with the long hours while trying to keep up my role within the family. Lynn told me about the changes that were happening. It turned out that if I was to train to consultant level in A&E, I could do this part time and she helped me organise this with the deanery.

I had just two months to go in my full time job when I became unwell at the end of 1993. I was exhausted when I realised I had started to have some symptoms of depression and went to see my GP. Over a short period, a matter of weeks, I had become low, was tearful from time to time and lacked energy and drive. In addition to this my sleep was disturbed and I had begun to wake up much earlier than I needed to. The GP started me on an antidepressant and reassured me that the medicine would start to work within a few weeks. I also approached the other consultant I worked for in A&E. He made sure that I was referred to the 'sick doctors' counselling service'. But after a short time of persisting at work, I went off sick, although everyone concerned felt sure that this dip in mood would respond to the drugs. After all I was soon to be part time and that would be such a great relief with not so many weekends, nights or evening shifts either. Lynn visited me at home and she talked enthusiastically about my return to work as a 'flexible trainee' – the term given to those of us who would train part time and we were to be supernumerary. At last I was going to be able to spend more time with Phil and the children, attend to their activities much more and still be able to train to consultant level in my new found career.

2: The Reality of Mental Illness

My attitude towards mental health problems changed when it happened to me. I was sure I had a mild illness and I knew that I wasn't a weak character. Unlucky yes, but I didn't think I was to blame to begin with. At that time, we all felt sure it was related to my heavy work hours and so, once I started to work part time we believed it would all be over.

When I had worked in one of the Southampton hospitals, it was right next door to the department of psychiatry, known as the DOP (pronounced by its capital letters). I accompanied my registrar to see a patient over there and had felt uneasy just at the thought of seeing someone who was mentally ill. I don't know exactly why as I had really enjoyed my psychiatry attachment as a student and got an 'A' for it, but that was at least ten years previously. What exactly was I afraid of? Did I think it might be catching? Mental illness was something that happened to other people, not those who were as smart and strong as I was. Those who came into A&E having overdosed or self harmed in other ways were felt to be feeble, time wasters, attention seekers. It was always a cry for help; if we judged that they really did want to commit suicide they were given a bit more sympathy. The over-riding feeling was that you shouldn't be nice to them though as they would only do it again if you were. How wrong I was to have embraced such attitudes.

I was therefore disappointed when it turned out that the 'sick doctors' counselling service' I had been referred to was to take place in this very building, the DOP. I did not consider myself to be a psychiatric patient.

At church, I had a mixed experience. Some friends with the best of intentions told me that my eyes were not truly focused on the Lord, I was not coming close enough to Him, I wasn't spending enough time in prayer and I wasn't reading the Bible enough. I know that these things were not said to discourage me, but the consequence was to confirm to myself what I already thought – that I had become a second rate Christian.

The other response I encountered was 'shall we pray about this?' – then a fairly superficial prayer was said. Others just smiled sympathetically and said they would pray for me. I know now that this is quite common for sufferers and it is just because people genuinely don't know how to react. I don't suppose I would have done any better. But I felt isolated and unsure and so became much more determined to get over this depression as quickly as possible. However I did have some friends who just accepted me how I was and I really appreciated their kindness and listening ears.

I managed to get through Christmas somehow and I'm not sure whether we had one of our usual New Year's Eve parties that year but soon, two months had passed. My part time job was due to start but I was not getting better; if anything I was feeling worse. I realised that no amount of 'trying' would make me feel any better. I couldn't seem to pull myself together.

I felt so low, the darkness was almost tangible. I kept myself shut in the bedroom except for when the children came home from school. I barely talked to Phil and at that time did not share with him what I was feeling. The initial tears had dried up and my emotions went numb apart from a growing fear and anxiety that I was never going to get out of this. The once rosy future looked grey and ugly as indeed my life had become. I was forever tired and had no energy; even normal movements felt heavy and protracted, described aptly as though 'wading through treacle'. Despite the absolute fatigue, I could not sleep. I found that I could not get to sleep and then, when I did, I would wake in the early hours and lie there with my mind as active as my body was tired. My thoughts took on a life of their own; I was a complete failure, I had brought this on myself, I was a bad person. I felt ashamed and I was to blame. Even my secure foundation that Jesus had died on the cross to save me from my sins could not take away the dreadful guilt I felt. I was a bad Christian; everything the people at church had said to me was true. I couldn't get any comfort from prayer; I couldn't read the Bible as I couldn't concentrate. I was totally self absorbed by my pain and the depths of my despair. I didn't know where to turn and then the thoughts started coming to me that life wasn't worth living. I was a bad wife, Phil would be better off without me. I started trying to imagine who he could marry to take care of the children. But that was it, the children! They needed a mummy even if she was bad. Anyway they wouldn't know how I felt as I was able to put a smile on and pretend that I was ok. It was easier for everyone if they didn't know.

But my desperation became unbearable and the desire to commit suicide grew stronger. I was being tortured by the pain in the depths of my being; there was no relief, no hope for the future and my mind persisted in telling me that death was the only way out of it. I rang the only person I knew that I thought might understand; my friend Janet. She was also a doctor but worked in psychiatry. Our husbands knew each other as, like Phil, Jeremy also swapped roles and became the househusband. When I told her what was going on, she took matters into her own hands and took me to the GP. I admitted my suicidal thoughts and the GP realised that this was serious. When we got back home, Phil had then to accompany me to an emergency appointment back at the DOP.

The doctor I saw there asked Phil to take me home only to get packed. He insisted that I needed to be admitted to hospital and, because I was working in Southampton, this had to be 'out of area'. Phil took me to the Old Manor Hospital in

Salisbury. They gave me a single room, that's all I remember, apart from seeing him drive away while my tears were streaming down my face. What on earth had I done? Oh God, oh God I whispered. It all seemed wrong somehow and I felt afraid, responsible for the mess I was in and I thought I really shouldn't be there. The doctors I saw felt differently; to them I was a legitimate psychiatric patient and slowly I came to accept that.

The next memory is when the doctor told me that I needed ECT. As a doctor I had never seen it done, just heard that it works. But it was still a shock to find that it was being offered to me. I was reassured when it was explained to me that I would feel nothing; I was to have a short general anaesthetic so I would be asleep through the whole procedure. If I developed a headache afterwards, I would be given painkillers. My recovery would be a lot quicker than waiting weeks while more and different drugs were tried. I wanted to get better quickly, so, despite my initial fears, I readily agreed and signed the consent form. But this was just the beginning.

It is actually so good that we can't see into the future. I had no way of knowing that my admission to the psychiatric hospital in Salisbury was the first to come of many admissions to hospital. I had a course of ECT and then I was much better, but that was all relative. I was discharged home on a new set of medication but I was still far from well. I could function on my own, but not for long. I soon deteriorated again. I had accepted that I was now mentally ill and realised that hospital was not so very frightening because it was a place of refuge; refuge from life and all its demands. I was not visited by friends though – for a start, Salisbury was about 45 minutes by car from Southampton, but also I think that they didn't quite know what to do or say. Neither was I sent any 'Get Well' cards which you would normally expect to receive if you were admitted to hospital for some time. My parents were nearby so they came to visit me and so did Phil when he could.

Fortunately Phil being at home meant that the children were well catered for, but I missed them and they missed me. I remember little from those times as my depression was so severe that my memory was impaired. ECT can also affect the memory, but I have a global deficit for those years which is more to do with the illness than just the ECT treatment.

Life Ongoing

Basically a pattern started of admission and ECT followed by discharge home and then trials of different drugs in different combinations followed by a further admission. I continued to have psychotherapy from Ian when I was at home; the person I had been referred to from the sick doctors' counselling service. This still took place at the DOP, but I was no longer afraid of the building. I found him very understanding and helpful, although I remember very little of the content of those sessions.

My thoughts of going back to work had to be well and truly shelved and the all pervading hopelessness took an increasing reign on my life. Since a year had now passed, I was no longer eligible for 'sick pay' and was started on benefits. This meant that Phil had a new mountain to climb; money for bills like the mortgage had stopped coming in and he realised that he needed to find work. After so many years out of work this was not easy, but eventually he was offered a programming job in Guildford, 50 miles from home. I looked after myself and the children as best I could while I was at home, but I was not really managing well as I had so little energy and I was neglecting the housework amongst other things. I had been assigned a social worker and he decided that I needed help. Social services sent in a carer who came every day while Phil was at work. I remember sitting on the sofa in our dining room and wishing I didn't feel I had to talk to her; she was absolutely lovely but I felt so much distress and anguish yet felt I must cover it up, so tried chatting just normally. Then I wondered whether she would think I shouldn't have a carer. I was so deeply unsure about every aspect of life. I was thankful that friends and family rallied round and helped to take and collect the children from school but once again thought I didn't deserve it. After all, I was responsible for my condition – or so I believed.

Unfortunately I deteriorated again and became a danger to myself once more, so I was readmitted to hospital as was the pattern of this illness. During the admissions Phil organised for our friends and family to continue the school run with the children and care for them until he got home; they were involved with various after school activities, so lifts for them had to be planned too. Praise God for all the help we received with meals prepared by doting Grandma and others, but basically Phil became very tired and says he spent a lot of his life on 'automatic' as he cared for our active, growing children, went to work and visited his very sick wife.

The medical services could give him no support towards his own welfare or the welfare of the children while I was in hospital and only a few close friends knew to what extent he was pouring out his life just to keep the family going. I was of course oblivious to this, too exhausted by my tortured mind to appreciate all the effort that was going on behind the scenes to keep the show on the road. It was just as well really. I was still tormented by the delusion that I was totally responsible for my condition, that I was not really ill, just the worst person in the world. My guilt was not relieved by any spiritual words and when I was able to get to church, I either felt nothing or was overwhelmed with tears when trying to join in with the praise and worship. I responded to any and every call for healing, but still nothing seemed to happen.

33

Mean time I was once again allowed home but I had started to self harm. This wasn't noticeable to others at first. My suicidal thoughts fluctuated but I kept thinking that if only I could die by 'natural' means then it would be better for the children. So I started inhaling the bags of hay we had for the guinea pigs. I knew that this would induce an asthma attack, so when nobody was around I would do this, but the acute shortness of breath I experienced, though severe, was not enough to fulfil my expectations.

Then on one memorable day, I picked up a razor blade; I cut up and down both my arms and Phil came home from work to find me covered in blood. However I refused to go to A&E. I knew how I would be treated if I turned up there, so my kind GP had a go at putting paper stitches on the worst of the cuts. Oh I do lament that day! I regret it so much, now I have the tell tale scars and they will be with me forever. Injuring myself took such a short time to complete and though I have been for a plastic surgery consultation I have been advised that there are too many scars to do anything to retrieve the situation. The scars were not something that even crossed my mind on that fateful day, but then nor was the possibility that I would ever be well again. I never attacked my arms again and I don't really know why I did it, except to 'try out pain' as some kind of relief for my mind.

The Prospect of Brain Surgery is Introduced

Soon I was no longer being admitted 'out of area'. The psychiatric teams involved had decided that it was highly unlikely that I would ever work again, so there was no reason now to treat me anywhere else. That meant I was admitted to the DOP. Not only that, there were times when I needed to be sectioned. I was under a specialist in mood disorders Professor

Chris Thompson who is now the Chief Medical Officer of the Priory Group. He had treated many patients with what was now true for me, 'treatment refractory depression', but he told us, years later, that he had never seen a case as severe as that which I displayed. After about five and a half years, with all the known drug combinations, many, many ECT treatments and twice weekly psychotherapy, I became permanently hospitalised. I had been burning myself with boiling water and attacked myself again with razor blades, inflicting serious injury that required emergency surgery for a potentially fatal wound. I was highly suicidal. I had lost all hope of ever recovering and realised for sure that my family would be better off without me, when Prof Thompson had another idea. He was talking about a more radical solution, still unfortunately controversial, brain surgery – neurosurgery for mental disorder or NSMD. I remember feeling stunned. I had never even heard there was such a treatment. He was very reassuring that the modern operation was highly specific and very safe. What I did not know was that he and his successor Dr David Baldwin had realised that my prognosis was that I would die if nothing else could be done. The surgery was regarded as a last resort treatment and only took place in specialised centres after prolonged assessment. Prof Thompson gave us time to think over his suggestion and, despite my initial shock, both Phil and I agreed that anything was worth a try. So I was then moved onto the waiting list to be seen at the Maudsley Hospital in London for assessment.

There was fierce opposition from my psychotherapist; Ian had left and I was being seen by a lady who I liked very much but she was sure that brain surgery would not help me. She still believed the key could be found in psychotherapy even though I had been seeing either herself or Ian regularly for the last five and a half years. My sister looked on the internet to find out about brain surgery and warned me of grave dangers – these turned out to be unfounded, such is the negative press towards NSMD. For instance the operation was described in a similar light to the old lobotomies, as giving you personality changes, as being barbaric, inflicting brain damage on a perfectly normal brain. The truth is, the severely depressed brain is not perfectly normal at all. (Ongoing research shows structural changes to an area in the brain called the hippocampus, which are not present in non-depressed brains.) Nor is the operation barbaric, and it does not change your personality, not by a little bit, not at all except to restore a normal person from a severely depressed one! Medicine has moved on a long way since the times portrayed in the film *One Flew over the Cuckoo's Nest*.

Prof Thompson duly moved on to another post and I was handed over to Dr Baldwin – both of these men, like all the psychiatrists I had seen, were extraordinarily kind. Although I didn't see the consultants that often – once a week at the most while I was in hospital – they always treated me with dignity and respect.

I found the atmosphere on the wards at the DOP extremely difficult. The conditions were not conducive to recovery. There was nothing for me to do except sit in the day room with fellow patients of both sexes and all manner of different conditions. At times it could be frightening when someone very disturbed would 'kick off' and all the staff would rush in to calm them down. There would be swearing and fighting and sometimes the furniture got thrown. No it was not good. The television was always on but I rarely watched it, as I didn't like what was on and was not one of those patients who dominated the remote control! I helped to do the washing up after our cups of tea, which were served from a trolley at various times through the day, but I still felt absolutely dreadful and longed for some relief from my pervasive depressive thoughts, which continued unabated. Unfortunately I did come across some very negative attitudes towards me from a minority of nurses, who labelled me with their own diagnoses of personality disorders – despite the fact that this was not upheld by any of the doctors. These particular individuals felt that the fact that I wasn't responding to treatment had to be an indication that I 'enjoyed' being ill; that I had some purpose or underlying gain from my condition. They let me know what they thought even though they could not articulate what exactly it was I gained from being ill or why on earth I would feel that the belittling existence of being locked on a psychiatric ward could possibly be preferable to my life with a loving husband and four children and my aspirations to train as a consultant in Emergency Medicine. I was too depressed to argue but I felt it keenly. I really needed empathy and kindness but received the very opposite and I felt I was being punished.

It happened in small ways, like when the staff knew I liked a bed by the window and since I was a long stay patient that was not an unreasonable request; but time and again, when I went out on leave, it would be taken away from me and I was placed in a nearby bed instead, my belongings all jumbled up in a bag. Even though this was relatively trivial, it made an enormous difference to me as I used to sit by the window and look out for a lot of the day as I wasn't allowed out by myself. I was accused of supplying razor blades to other patients so they could copy my self harm, which I would never do. I was mortified by that charge – it was difficult enough obtaining them for myself and I had no wish that anyone else would be harmed in any way. My defence always seemed inadequate because, for a certain few, my delusions that I was a fraud were believed as true.

There was a certain solidarity amongst the patients against this harsh regime, as I was not the only one who had had such difficulties and we did look out for each other, even though in reality we had little to offer. We did make friends, though, and I really appreciated the company of certain women who were also in and out of hospital like me. But there were also some extremely kind and understanding nurses who went out of their way to reassure me and treat me with respect. My named nurse Karen in particular was very patient with me, allowing me to express myself, but carefully challenging my delusional thinking to try and counter my unkindness towards myself. Talking with an understanding person always made me feel a bit better, though its benefits would not last too long. Because of the self harm, whenever I came onto the ward I would be strip searched, which was humiliating; it mattered so much how this was done. I owe so much to these kind nurses, because, without them, my life would have been unbearable. I was no easy patient – it is always disheartening for both doctors and nurses when a patient does not improve, or, as in my case, continues to deteriorate. I managed to self harm despite the supposed safety of the ward. I think the Lord has given me much favour by providing good and understanding doctors, but I know from my experience of working that as a group, we also have some bad apples in the cart.

The doctors I happened to see were always very supportive; my only complaint was that I saw so little of them. The 'ward round' once a week was when we got to see the consultant and it was always in the company of a nurse and other members of the team, which was a little inhibiting. Sometimes the wait to be seen seemed endless and we would all sit in the day room anxiously waiting for our names to be called – it could take several hours and so if you were on the end of the list, it wasn't good. I could never settle during these times as it was during the ward round that important decisions were made, like a new regime of drugs or practical things like whether or not I would be allowed to go home at the weekend.

The Scottish Answer

Dr Baldwin learned that the Maudsley closed their neurosurgery unit down, but, before letting me know, he contacted the only other unit in the country, which was run by Professor Keith Matthews of the Advanced Interventions Service, in Dundee. He would be the psychiatrist in charge of my care. So though it was bad news, as I had been on a waiting list, Dr Baldwin was able to tell me that I had been referred to Dundee and the process was underway for me to receive treatment there.

It was in January of 2001 when Phil and I flew up to Scotland for me to be admitted to the Dundee psychiatric unit for assessment. I was writing a kind of diary at that time and noted that Prof Matthews was a 'very nice, sweet bloke'. He was in fact truly memorable; he looked like a rugby player, with a bald head and wearing a black tee-shirt, not the least bit like a psychiatrist! All the previous psychiatrists I had seen were in suits and ties, or the ladies in smart clothes. I did not appreciate his amazing charisma at the time. But his assessment was that I was a suitable candidate for surgery. I did have to have further interviews with the Health Commissioners to check I was agreeing to this of my own free will, as you can never be forced to have treatment of this kind. I was on a Section at that time, so I was not in hospital out of my own choice, therefore it was doubly important that these checks were made. One thing which Dr Baldwin kept to himself was that I could not have the operation without funding from the then PCT (Primary Care Trust). His team had quite a fight to persuade them that this treatment was a good option since I had spent four and a half years out of the last seven as an inpatient in their various hospitals, had received over 100 ECT treatments, was still being treated with all sorts of drug combinations and had psychotherapy twice a week. I am so grateful that they eventually agreed to fund the operation!

I felt that I had nothing to lose. I didn't actually believe the operation would work for me, such was my hopeless view on life, but I felt I should have tried everything as then I could end my life with a clear conscience. Such was some of the muddled thinking I exhibited. After the successful assessment for surgery, I was transferred to the Psychiatric Intensive Care Unit at the DOP, in order to keep me extra safe. I had a nurse assigned to observe me 24 hours a day and I did not have any privacy at all, not even when going to the toilet. I preferred being on this ward despite the restrictions on me; the nurses were so kind and there was more activity provided. I could stay in my room if I chose and sleep whenever I wanted, but was encouraged to do things and it was here that I started doing jigsaws, which gave me some distraction. There was also a small garden and it did me good to be able to sit in the sunshine during the summer.

I did not know that a new prayer group had formed specifically to pray for me. This was a group of dedicated individuals from different churches as well as our own, most of whom I had never met, but who had faith that God could change this hopeless situation and they prayed for my healing. It reminds me of the situation described in the Gospels, when four friends took their paralysed friend on his mat, to the feet of Jesus. There was no room, so they dug a hole in the roof to lower him down and Jesus commended them for their faith. I was like the paralysed man, helpless and lacking in any faith. This prayer group were those four friends. They did indeed bring me to the feet of Jesus. They believed that the operation I was to have was right and would provide the key to unlock the door to my freedom. One of them, a lady called Chris Larkin, (though neither Phil nor I had met her at the time), had a prophecy that the operation would give me the ability to make a decision; she did not know any more than that. I continued to know nothing of this group praying, because Phil kept it from me. By this stage in the illness, I hated being prayed for as I felt that the answer never happened and I used to feel that I had let the pray-ers down as I could not provide them with the answers to their prayers. I had not lost my faith in God, I knew He was there and I was looking forward to meeting Jesus in heaven when I died by suicide.

3: Time for Deliverance

When the time of the operation had come, I was escorted by two nurses, as I was flown up to Scotland to their brand new psychiatric unit, the Carseview Centre, located at Ninewells Hospital in Dundee. Professor Matthews went through the details of the operation which the neurosurgeon, Mr Eljamel, would perform, the risks, which are unfortunately present in all surgery of any nature, and also the details of the expected recovery. Research then had shown that certain results could be expected. Everyone would require nine months to a year of further therapy including CBT (cognitive behaviour therapy) and continuation of drug treatments, it was at the end of this that it could be determined whether you were part of the third who made a good recovery from the illness, the third who improved or the third who were not helped. (These statistics have been updated now and 50–60% of patients are expected to make a good recovery from their illness.)

The operation was nothing like the notorious and awful lobotomies, which were famous for being performed on mentally ill patients in the past. This operation was very discreet; a specifically placed lesion in the anterior cingulate of the brain. It would be done under MRI (a type of scanner) guidance – this is very similar to operations done for intractable Parkinson's disease. It is thought that this interrupts some of the abnormal neural pathways which are occurring in the kind of severe treatment resistant depression that I had.

The operation went well, but I was pretty fed up after the surgery, even though I had been warned that nothing would happen immediately and even though I had little belief that I would respond anyway; I now had to contend with the recovery and so far all I experienced was the worst headache in my life, fever and a swollen face. However these symptoms were settling down. I still had a nurse watching me for 24 hours a day, so it is no surprise that she sat next to me as I went to sit in one of the day rooms. One of the other patients, who I had got to know a bit, came in and sat down. She had been out for the day and said, 'all I want is to be at home with my husband and children'. I was not feeling well deposed towards anyone that evening, as I was feeling particularly low and irritable, so my unkind reaction, which remained unspoken, was 'oh just shut up!'. But at that very instant, a light switched on inside my head and I felt it fill with light; I heard myself echo her – 'all I want is to be at home with my husband and children' but for me this was a joyous statement. Tears streamed down my cheeks in relief; my depression had lifted! As I rose to go to my room, another thought came into my mind, 'what about the self harm?'. I talked to it as though it were a voice and said, 'I don't want self harm anymore'.

I believe that was the vital decision which Chris Larkin's prophecy referred to and, for the next few days, I was to repeat that response to the self harm thoughts as they entered my mind. Within three days the thoughts had gone, and I had no more thoughts of self harm. This had all occurred on day eight following the operation – long before the projected time for recovery.

Free at Last

I was rejoicing and happy for the first time in seven years, but at the same time was confused and wary. How was I going to explain this to Professor Matthews? Would it last? I suddenly became aware of my predicament. I was sectioned in a mental hospital, 600 miles from home. How was I going to get out of here? The nursing staff were very sceptical of my instant recovery at first, but continued to support me. Thankfully Phil arrived from England and, with the Prof's permission, was able to take me out on day trips. I had phoned Phil before he left, but I didn't tell him about my recovery. However he knew by the tone of my voice that something very significant had happened. I was able to tell him face to face about it and he in turn told me about the prayer group and the prayers and prophetic words. I knew then that Jesus had healed me and I had to take our powerful, almighty God more seriously than I had ever done in my life.

Professor Matthews accepted my explanation of what had happened and saw the remarkable change in me but he remained cautious. An early response to surgery had not been seen before at that time and he counselled us that this may only be a temporary reaction. By then my healing had persisted for a good five days, not long I admit, but I was convinced that it was permanent. None of the doctors I saw, including those back in Southampton, could give us any explanation for what had happened, but thankfully on my return they saw and recognised my recovery as genuine.

I am no longer entirely unique. Another patient has since then also experienced the phenomenon of a light switching on, but theirs occurred at nine months after the operation. There has also been another early response to the surgery.

God's touch on my life remained; this was not temporary. I was able to walk out of the life that had been dominated by hospital, nurses and doctors. I had been an inpatient continuously for more than a year when I recovered. I was so confident of my healing that I refused further psychotherapy in the form of CBT, but this was after a session when the therapist admitted she did not know what to do since I had no symptoms or evidence of depressive thinking. I also weaned myself off the drugs even though the advice was to stay on them for at least a year. (Not something I would recommend in retrospect!) I was convinced that it was all over and I would never be depressed again. I wanted to get back to normal life as quickly as possible. I'm afraid I was at that time totally oblivious to the terrible trauma that Phil and the children had suffered over the years. I had never felt so alive and I expected everyone else to feel that way too.

The church rejoiced with me. I now understood that many of our friends had faithfully prayed, despite the fact that some of them told me that they could not cope with me being mentally ill, so had deliberately stayed away from me. I had the opportunity to give my testimony to a congregation of about 600 at church and people spoke of a miracle, and some appeared asking us to pray for them in the hope that the healing might somehow spread. I certainly had faith then that God could do anything, He had certainly done wonders through this operation, but I was rather impatient with those who were less sure.

A Steep Learning Curve

I did come back down to earth again though. I had to learn to get to know my husband and children again. In fact during the months following, Phil and I were to experience the worst year of our marriage. It was as if I had returned from the war. I could not understand why Phil remained so emotionally neutral; I felt that he should be leaping up and down with joy. I did not recognise just how hard his life had been. He had brought up our four children as if a single parent, working full time and also giving support to and visiting his terminally ill wife. I had made two serious suicide attempts and some of the self harm had left me really ill; he said he lived with the constant fear that one day he would get the phone call to say I was dead. He was totally exhausted and emotionally drained and on top of that it seemed that we scarcely agreed about anything and our conversations often erupted into arguments.

We also experienced the death of various friends during that year. We had invitations to six funerals and attended five. Tragically two young men that we knew had died by suicide, which was very poignant for us.

Our children had also suffered greatly, having been deprived of their mother's intimate involvement in their lives during their seven years of growing up. I had tried to be a 'good' mother to them during my illness and often was able to spend the school holidays at home, but the reality was that I was in no fit state to nurture and teach them let alone give them the emotional support that they needed. I had an illness which wasn't spoken of; our son Simon said that he knew that he couldn't talk of my illness to anyone at school. Friends and family had helped out the best they could, but it took me a long time to realise that I could not just step into the children's lives as though nothing had happened, as I had missed such vital years.

In fact it was only relatively recently that I came to realise that I seriously let my children down during that first year after my recovery. However God is gracious and when we fall down and make mistakes, He lifts us up again. However I have had to restore relationships and have needed to say sorry and ask for forgiveness.

My relationship with Phil was healed by the end of that initial year of my recovery, but before that happened things got so bad that I wondered whether we had a future together. We both had to return to first principles as it were and think about what we felt for each other when we had originally got together and realise that we really loved each other then. So what had changed? Yes, I had fallen out of love with him, but

46

slowly and surely the love returned for each other when we both expressed the bottom line of our marriage – 'I love you'. The bickering ceased and fortunately we came through the experience stronger and more in love with each other than we had ever been.

I know this story might grate for other couples not as fortunate as ourselves. We were the only couple on the neurosurgery for mental disorder programme who had survived without splitting up. Living with a severely depressed or mentally ill spouse is never easy and, with no hope of recovery, marriages and relationships are often a casualty. But the Lord has kept us. Phil had continued to love me despite my illness. The marriage vows which we took were 'for better, for worse, for richer, for poorer, in sickness and in health' and he surely demonstrated that he had meant what he had said.

A Note about Healing

The Lord God heals all the time, He made our bodies so that they self heal. It is so amazing that when I had cut myself, the wounds still healed – but that is what happens to any of us. We can describe the process by which it happens scientifically, indeed God created the world and therefore the rules that the world runs by. A gifted surgeon may operate, but she cannot cause the wounds to heal; a GP prescribes medicines for you to take, but he cannot make your body react to them so that recovery occurs. In the same way that a farmer sows seed and tends the crops, it is God who gives the growth. So the psychiatrist may give drugs or ECT, a neurosurgeon may operate on the brain, a psychotherapist or counsellor may teach new ways of thinking, but it is God who does the healing. I had all these treatments and it is God who made me well. Without His touch, we would all die. Do I deny God's extraordinary healing by prayer, anointing with oil or laying on of hands? Far be it from me to do so. Jesus heals yesterday, today and tomorrow and can do it without any help from doctors, nurses or therapists. I know of plenty of miraculous healings which have taken place. Indeed my own healing certainly seemed miraculous! God created the universe; He created nature's laws that govern the science behind the practice of medicine. So mental illness, like any illness, should be treated by medical or related professionals until you get better or such time as God heals, whether it occurs naturally, by prayer, by word of knowledge or by the laying on of hands.

My healing transformed my life. In fact two miracles seem to have taken place; not only was my depression completely lifted from my life but I was also set free from dependence on medical services and all that that entailed. I was effectively institutionalised when I was discharged from the DOP. As an inpatient for over a year I had been totally dependent on the hospital staff for all aspects of my physical life. The doctors and CPN (Community Psychiatric Nurse) wisely continued to support me for a time after my recovery, but even before they thought I was ready, I was the one to say 'enough is enough' and dispensed with their services!

I cannot take the credit for this. God had done an amazing thing in my life and, having experienced such a close touch from Him, I wanted to get as far away from the 'old' depressed way of life as I could.

It is 'by His wounds you have been healed' (1 Peter 2:24). Jesus healed me and I indeed testify to what God did in my life by His grace and the power of the Holy Spirit. However as I have mentioned, during the illness I became not just sceptical about people praying for me, but also wary. It wasn't like that to start with, I used to take every opportunity to get prayed for and I was hopeful of my healing, just as I was hopeful that medical interventions would work. In fact it was urgent as far as I was concerned because I really wanted to get back to my new part time job and take over my role in the home.

However it was not without difficulties. Friends had very good intentions for me, the sufferer of mental health problems. When I had the courage to share with people my emotional or psychological problems, then the immediate response of 'let's pray about it' was rarely helpful. I, like most people in this situation, wanted to be listened to. If the sharing took place within the context of a prayer time it was different, but it was as though I brought forth a panic reaction within friends which told them, 'I can't cope' or 'help, what am I going to say?' and as a result consciously or subconsciously they hoped a simple prayer would be the answer. Though I did believe that even then God was a God of miracles, and I was not trying to underestimate His power, it did feel as if this kind of response had more to do with their own discomfort rather than with me, the person who had shared. I learned from that that I must avoid superficial responses and prayers for instant healing, which allow me to neatly back away from the problem, when I am dealing with others in difficult circumstances.

From my own experience, and the experience of others, I have found that God chooses to heal miraculously on occasions but sometimes He doesn't. I am no longer surprised that more often than not the symptoms of emotional or mental health problems indicate either that God is doing something deeper in a sufferer or that, through the suffering, He desires a closer, more intimate walk with that person. I have read that some Christians who have mental health problems find that their soul remains totally well. I assume by this they mean that their spiritual life remains healthy, although if they develop negative depressive thinking, it must be jolly hard work – something I have learnt in more recent years, when I am *well enough* to 'fight' the thoughts and overwhelm *them* with biblical truth.

There may be issues in a person's past life or childhood that need to be explored and dealt with professionally by secular or Christian mental health workers such as counsellors or psychotherapists. Indeed they may require treatment from their GP, psychiatrist or cognitive behavioural therapist (CBT). But sometimes the right pastoral care may be enough, though this should not be assumed. It is not a decision that can be made easily by a lay person and it is vitally important that a mental illness is diagnosed, if present, and receives proper treatment, so a visit to the GP should be encouraged if there is any doubt.

4: An Identity Resolved

It is inevitable that some disabilities are, or become, part of our identity; this is evident in the Bible, for instance in the New Testament we see the leper (Mark 14:3) and the blind and the lame (Matt 21:14). In those days a leper was seen as 'unclean' and was therefore not allowed to associate with those who were clean. He or she would have to ring a bell as they came near other people and shout 'unclean, unclean'. However these descriptions of disabilities also partly reflected the lifelong nature of these problems and in a time when there was no modern medicine and no hope of cure (until Jesus came), the label stuck. But isn't it wonderful when the disability is not what springs to mind when you speak of a friend, or a brother or sister who belongs to your church and suffers with a particular affliction?

There is also the question of how we see ourselves. Do we see ourselves first and foremost as our problem? Or do we see ourselves first and foremost how we are redefined when Jesus saves us and the Father adopts us into his family?

Let me try it. I am Cathy; I'm a child of God. I'm very precious – Jesus died on the cross for me. I am much loved by God, friends and family. That's not boasting, it's fact and doesn't it feel good? Then I might go on to describe myself by my different roles in life or circumstances that I am in and at the end I might even be brave enough to say 'and by the way, I suffer from severe depression'. But I may choose to leave it out, as I don't want to be treated as though I have such a difficulty. However, because I have a vision which includes the desire to de-stigmatise mental illness, and it explains quite a lot about my life, I think I will choose to keep it in.

Now some conditions seem more acceptable within society and the Church, while some are simply not, despite the fact that no condition is purely physical or purely psychological. For instance it seems okay to talk about chronic fatigue syndrome, (some people call it ME), diabetes or asthma, even though the evidence is that the former is a brain disorder and the fact that psychological factors have a huge part to play in the management of chronic physical disease. Some people 'just get on with it', which we all admire, others cannot. For some reason people forget to take their vital medications, or don't stick to a diet or carry on smoking against advice and their illnesses become worse and dominate their lives more than they could or should do. Am I judgemental when they experience an exacerbation to their illness? I certainly think I have been in the past, which I thoroughly regret.

Society for decades has made fun of the mentally ill. It is still in keeping with political correctness to tell jokes about mental illness – 'the nutter who lives down the road'. Everyone laughs but at whose expense? Yes I laugh too but inwardly I groan knowing that for the unspoken minority, this could be so offensive were it to be told in their hearing. I hear the young describing someone as absolutely 'mental', which I know is a term of endearment, but I can't help wondering how they would have described me when I was in the midst of a severe depressive episode.

René Descartes is often credited with being the 'Father of Modern Philosophy' and brought back the concept that we are divided into mind and body. But we are whole people, we are not split into mind, body, soul or spirit – each part of our makeup is inextricably linked and the artificial divisions into physical and mental acceptable to medical science are not scriptural, nor were they part of the philosophy among believers of the Early Church. So in Jesus' day there would not have been the divide between physical and mental illness – and Jesus healed all who were sick.

In the Church of today, I see all manner of tolerance but sometimes all manner of judgement is taking place and I include myself as being guilty of this. I would say that by and large 'physical complaints' are treated with more sympathy than mental illness. This is probably because the latter remains frightening and poorly understood. Perhaps it is less common for a prayer meeting to be called in order to pray for healing or support for a church member with a mental illness than for someone newly diagnosed with cancer. Ah, you might think, but mental illness doesn't kill you, but I know from my own story that that isn't true. There is evidence that the psychological effects, or even depression, can cause far more suffering for a person with heart disease or cancer than the physical illness itself. Also, far from being benign, mental illness can kill a person by causing them to self harm or commit suicide. It may also shorten their lives by making them generally more vulnerable to all sorts of illnesses and disabilities. Patients with major mental illnesses must now have a medical examination once a year in recognition of their propensity to develop physical illnesses which might otherwise go unnoticed.

Sometimes when the identity of a person includes their condition or disability it can be helpful, but surely it can also trap that person in their illness? I wouldn't have wanted to be known by my illness, 'put into a box' or branded by a label. The condition can become the prime influence in their lives, so, if healing is sought, faith has to be present not only for the healing of the disorder but also actually for the person involved to live a new life without the influence of the condition. It may well have brought them a degree of stability, even security to their life. This is true for all manner of conditions and illnesses.

It can be frightening to live without the extra support of a spouse, your family or your friends; without the routine of hospital or GP visits, without the care of doctors, nurses, social workers or therapists and without extra support from your pastor and the knowledge of friends praying for you. Suddenly you may have to work and no longer are you excused from volunteering for the inevitable tasks that need to be done at home or even within your church. If this is not resolved, the healed person may soon succumb to the same thing again or to another illness or disorder.

More Faith Required

I had to give up my financial support in the way of benefits. I had been receiving the equivalent of Incapacity Benefit and Disabled Living Allowance. Phil had had to remortgage the house during my illness; such was the sorry state of our finances. With this in mind, it was hard to write to the Benefits Agencies and refuse the money. I also had to get a job; that was scary too. Phil had had a dream that he believed the Lord had given him. It was that I would go back to Emergency Medicine (A&E) and start back where I had left off. I hadn't practiced medicine for almost eight years! I did not like this dream and initially I tossed aside this notion that it was from God; I couldn't see myself back at work, particularly in the emergency department at Southampton General that had treated me on numerous occasions for episodes of self harm. I knew all about the stigma associated with mental illness, but even more so for self harm. I had experienced the cruelty of some of the staff as a result of my behaviour. In particular, I remembered how one of the surgeons who was called to see me, when I had deeply cut into my abdomen, had no qualms at hurting me as he explored the wound without local anaesthetic. Of course at the time I, like him, thought that I was getting what I justly deserved.

Yet the Lord gave me the courage. I came round and listened to Him as He whispered to me that I was a child of God, that I had had an illness which caused me to do such bizarre things to myself, but now I was better. He enabled me to enter that very same Emergency department holding my head up high and begin preparations for a return to work there. All blessings, honour and power belong to Him!

That didn't mean I did not feel nervous. The very first day that I was to spend as an observer there, my heart was racing and I had to keep saying to myself, over and over, 'I am God's child. I was ill, now I'm better. I have nothing to be ashamed of.' I literally felt like Daniel in the lion's den, I thought I would be eaten alive! In fact, my fears were largely unfounded; thankfully most of the doctors had moved on. But I did have to put up with some funny looks as nurses tried to recall where on earth they had seen me before and there was a nursing sister who had known me from both before my illness and during it. She took several days before she addressed me directly, saying 'It's good to have the old Cathy back'. For a few nurses, it took a while longer to accept me being back as part of the team, working as a doctor.

This part of my story is good news indeed; God can do anything through ordinary people like you and me, even when we suffer from the most extreme and serious mental illness. The Bible even says so: 'I can do all things through Him who strengthens me' (Philippians 4:13 NASB).

Who Gets Depressed?

When I first became depressed, I took myself to see my GP, but I did have the advantage of a medical training, so I recognised it for what it was. However even doctors can fail to recognise the symptoms of mental illness within themselves. Part of the denial that goes on is caused by the stigma; no one likes to admit that they could be mentally ill, just as I had failed to. It sounds so permanent, though the reality is that 1 in 4 of us will suffer with some form of mental illness at some time in our lives, however transiently. To be mentally ill may be associated in some people's minds with weakness of character or instability, although clearly this is not true. Some people think it's not a 'proper' illness, which is again untrue.

As I have mentioned before, sadly in Christian circles some people think that Christians should not get depressed. It was so helpful for me to know that biblical characters like Elijah, David and Job suffered from depression and also to have read of such famous Christians as Spurgeon, J.B. Phillips and Mother Teresa suffering too.

David, a man after God's heart, was anointed king over Israel, yet he expresses himself vividly in the psalms:

Turn to me and be gracious to me, for I am lonely and afflicted. The troubles of my heart have multiplied; free me from my anguish. Look upon my affliction and my distress and take away all my sins. Psalm 25:16–18

In another psalm David states, 'The Lord is close to the broken-hearted and saves those who are crushed in spirit.' (Psalm 34:18)

Elijah, after performing amazing miracles where he called down fire on his offering having drenched it and surrounded it by water and then slaying the prophets of Baal, became afraid when he had a death threat from the woman Jezebel. He sits under a tree and prays that he might die: 'I have had enough Lord, take my life, I am no better than my ancestors.' (1 Kings 19:4)

Chapter 3 of Job is the narrative of his lament where he curses the day he was born, then goes on to say:

For sighing comes to me instead of food, my groans pour out like water. What I feared has come upon me; what I dreaded has happened to me. I have no peace, no quietness; I have no rest, but only turmoil.

C.H. Spurgeon was a famous preacher from the 19th century and was said to have preached to over 10 million people in Britain. He suffered with long lasting depression after he preached to a large crowd in the Surrey Gardens Music Hall, where someone shouted 'fire'; in the rush of the people to evacuate the building seven died. Spurgeon was devastated and for weeks retreated into isolation. That was the start of his depression, yet he became able to continue with his life's work of being a pastor, preacher and founder not only of Spurgeon's college in London, but also of an orphanage for the homeless children of London.

Mother Teresa did not talk about her depression, but the publication of her letters after her death make it clear that not only did she suffer doubts about her faith in God, (which are common experiences for many believers), but also profound symptoms of depression. This is a quote from one of her letters: 'I am told God lives in me -- and yet the reality of darkness and coldness and emptiness is so great that nothing touches my soul.' Today, many other pastors and ministers suffer with depression, which is not surprising as they have the same life experiences as non-ordained people. Billy Graham's daughter Ruth Graham is another example; her depression has caused her to run conferences and write on the subject.

Another attitude that I came across on my recovery is the thinking that a person with mental illness is possessed. There is evidence in the Bible of demon possession being present in physical disorders as well (Luke 13:16). Yet, I have never come across this stance occurring for a person suffering with a physical problem with the exception of epilepsy. Seeing demon possession in a person suffering from mental illness has been responsible for the diabolical treatment of patients in the past. This can be very damaging for sufferers with any problem and the subject should be handled with care. I will explore this issue further in a later chapter.

5: A Question about Blame

Even though initially I did not hold myself responsible for my illness, it was not long before I very much blamed myself – even to an obsessive degree. It became part of my depressive thinking but, once I was better, I was able to disown that theory. However it is easy to blame the mentally ill for their illnesses, as it is easy to misunderstand that what is expressed is to do with personal failure. We also hold people liable who suffer with certain physical disorders eg obesity and diabetes or smoking and lung cancer – how many times have you heard, or thought yourself: 'no wonder, he is overweight' or 'she brought it on herself'. But the trouble with blaming someone with any illness, apart from being plain unkind and hypocritical, is that, like me, the sufferer most probably blames themselves and feels guilty already. This is not good or helpful and for any condition, certainly with depression, guilt feeds into any accompanying low self esteem and therefore makes the problem worse. Though guilt can be a motivator, it is never a healthy one unless of course it is the Spirit led conviction that leads to repentance and forgiveness. But the kind of guilt I am talking about, a feeling of blame, culpability or responsibility, which we may carry around with ourselves, is one of the things that Jesus died to set us free from. I need to remind myself of this regularly and how better than in Noel Richards' poignant song.

You laid aside your majesty,
Gave up everything for me,
Suffered at the hands of those you had created.

Is it with some of the attitudes I have mentioned that the
belief comes that someone suffering from a mental health
problem can 'just snap out of it' or 'pull themselves together'?
Any person may be able to do so if they suffer a transient or
superficial episode of normal sadness or melancholia. It
definitely doesn't work for a sufferer of mental illness, which
is totally beyond a person's control. Basically if you could snap
out of it, you would and if you can snap out of it, it's not a
mental illness! That is not to say that I could not present
myself differently to suit the occasion, (which is true for all of
us). When you are clinically depressed, it is still possible to
laugh or enjoy an event – it often leads to profound guilt and
doubt, making you feel that you are not actually suffering
from depression at all.

This was definitely my experience; I would spend a good
deal of time and effort in hiding the appearance of my illness. I
used to put on a 'front' or a 'mask', so that I would not pull
others down, but also to protect myself from hurtful
comments. I did this as much as I could at home as I thought
that this was better for the children. However, as a result of
this, my father used to say to me that he could not see
anything wrong with me. We discussed this after my recovery
and he said that he thought it would encourage me, but in fact
it did quite the reverse; I felt very hurt and imagined he
thought I was a fraud, which, considering my own doubts as
to the validity of my illness, made my mood drop even lower
if that were possible. I had a really good talk with both my
parents while I was working on my first book *Life after*

Darkness, which resolved the misunderstandings that had occurred between us during my illness.

Kind Words Meant Well

As I have described during the early days of the depression, there were plenty of people who wanted to help me and I listened to their counsel. I received instructions like 'you should get closer to God', 'you should read the Bible more' or 'you should pray more'. It was so difficult because I didn't know how to get closer to God, I couldn't concentrate to read the Bible more and my prayers were reduced to sighs and groaning. But I have found myself wondering whether these instructions would be said to someone suffering from a physical ailment too. The answer has come from a friend of mine who had cancer; she also had a similar experience while she was ill, so obviously this is not just confined to the realms of mental health. Suddenly I found my spiritual life was subject to scrutiny by people who I barely knew and she experienced the same thing.

I do want my Christian life to be examined by a Christian who is further on in the journey than I am. However I realise now that it can be a grave error to assume a person's problems are purely spiritual and more so that I am the one to fix them. This is not to say that a person's emotional or mental health problem is never spiritual, on the contrary a spiritual element may well be present, but Jesus' words 'first remove the log from your own eye, then you may see clearly to remove the speck from your brother's eye' (Matthew 7:5), is pure wisdom.

Now I face a new battle. I am no longer working again and am medically retired. This is after another bout of serious depression. Suffice it to say, my recovery has not been instant this time! It has been a slow recovery with significant 'down' periods occurring at intervals. I have had to come to terms with the fact that I now have to be on lifelong antidepressants, to try and prevent further relapses, and this needs to be supervised by a psychiatrist. I have to look after myself in other ways too. My stress resistance has gone down – a feature of the sort of depression I have experienced, which means it takes less to trigger a relapse. I have to exercise, to eat healthily, but the best bit of all is when I do suffer stress, I have to deliberately participate in activities that I find pleasant and I do have to avoid unnecessary stress. This involves real discipline for me. My psychiatrist is adamant that the reason I remain well is because I am not working and now have a relatively stress free life. However I do not want to allow myself to be bound by his words; I want to experience complete healing, but for now I believe that the Lord would have me follow the professor's advice.

I am determined that I will not let this disorder define my life. I sleep excessively because of the medication, but I do not have to make that an issue. If I cannot sleep for a day or even a number of days, then I will catch up in my own time, but it will not stop me living life to the full, within the boundaries that I have talked about – which were issued by my immensely kind and wise psychiatrist Professor Matthews.

Stereotyping is Not Helpful

Ideally a pre-requisite to recovery is that a sufferer should cut off their unhealthy dependence on their illness as part of their identity, but friends, family and their church must do the same. (I know it is possible to have our identity in other things too which can be equally unhealthy, such as our job or our social position.) Talking to friends who are also suffering from a mental illness, it is others' attitudes towards them that is often the most difficult thing to shift.

When I recovered from the years of my first episode of depression, I found that some people within our church did not appear to cope with me being well. We tend to put people 'in boxes', or stereotype people, not just because of an illness; it also occurs by race, by gender, by age for instance and is a feature of our Western society. I found that a few certain people were particularly prone to asking me how I was – not in the usual way – 'How are you?' anticipating a superficial answer like 'I'm fine thank you'. Instead they would ask slowly with an almost whining voice and a grimace of concern on their faces as if expecting a negative answer. This was not helpful to me. I had given my testimony at a Sunday morning meeting of my recovery and healing. I needed to be treated as just me, a well person. Funnily enough those same people had steered well clear of me when I was ill, basically illustrating the stigma of mental illness. This was not just a feature of our particular church – I have heard of the very same thing happening elsewhere and of course not necessarily within a church setting.

Some people have said that others' 'illness perception' of them is one of the hardest challenges to overcome.

There is always an exception to the rule though. A friend of mine named Susie has embraced her Bipolar disorder; it's very much part of her. But rather than feeling sorry for herself or bemoaning her lot, she has used it to reach out to others, particularly those with mental health problems. She really serves them. She organises events for the bipolar group in her locality, with whom she meets regularly. She befriends the lost and those who are alone. She brings people to church and, by her initiative, certainly one young woman has been saved and I am certain she has sown seeds in countless other's hearts. Suzie is not prejudiced, she is not proud, rather with cheerfulness and with little recognition carries out her God given ministry. What a shining example she is to me. Susie supported me when I was ill and admits she found it hard to cope with me when I was better. I, in turn, did not appreciate that her illness gave her the gateway into other vulnerable people's lives. I had the audacity to tell her to seek healing, which I had absolutely no right to do; she had and has plenty of opportunity within her church to ask for healing prayer, but the last thing she needs is to be pushed into it by someone who is following their own ideals rather than listening to God.

Life was Looking Good

By a year after my dramatic recovery from the first episode of depression, family life had taken on a sort of normality. Three of our children still lived at home and I was working part time in Southampton General Hospital Emergency Department as a junior doctor. I was off all medication and had no reason to be concerned with my mental health. I started to study for exams to take me up to the next grade in my career as an A&E doctor. The family were very tolerant with me as I spent time revising and within a fairly short time I was rewarded with a few more letters after my name: the membership of the faculty of A&E medicine or MFAEM. It had been really hard work for me, but the future looked rosy and I looked forward to the day when I would become a consultant in an Emergency Department. The children were growing up fast and were taking different courses in their own studies. Life was good. I interviewed and was accepted as a Specialist Registrar in A&E and started work at Portsmouth's Queen Alexandra Hospital.

Around the same time, I met with the CEO of a charity called Primhe, who promote education of the medical profession about mental illness. He heard my story and suggested that I write a book. He also asked whether I minded him mentioning it to others. Of course, I was delighted and said I had no objections. I did not expect to get any feedback, but, rather to my surprise, the editor of Radcliffe Publishing, Gillian Nineham, contacted me. She visited me and, though she had seen none of my writing, she offered me a contract to write my story. The idea had been suggested to me by others, but, more than ever, I realised that God had His hand on this; it was literally a God given opportunity. I agreed to the proposal and soon I started to research my medical and nursing notes to be able to write my book *Life after Darkness*. I had written a diary for the last 18 months of my illness, so, despite my severe memory loss, I was able to use that and the substance of the doctors' letters to be able to describe what kind of state I was in. Radcliffe is a secular publisher so I was able to share my testimony and it was seen by many people of all types of beliefs. I was also privileged to have the forewords written by two of my doctors and the book was published in January 2006.

More on Stigma

While I was writing, I used to take a notebook into work with me. It was small and discreet and I used to try and record verbatim any stigmatising comments I heard to give reality to what I was writing as, by then, I realised just how alive and well the stigma surrounding mental health is.

I am not wanting to be judgemental towards people who say stigmatising things; most of the time, it is done out of ignorance and the person who makes such remarks will not have thought at all that their words could possibly be hurting anyone. I am not perfect and own up to making many unkind and thoughtless comments during my life. I just want to be realistic about what I am saying. Laughing at 'the mad' has a long history and is not thought of as offensive. Recently I received a round robin email saying: 'Don't let your worries get the best of you; Moses started out as a basket case!'

A basket case refers directly to the activity of mentally ill patients as the Occupational Therapy departments used to involve them in activities such as, literally, making baskets. Also I have heard familiar comments such as 'she's off her rocker' or 'the men in white coats might take you away'.

As someone who has indeed been taken away, not by men in white coats but rather an ambulance crew, I am not personally offended by such comments, but when I think about it, they are very unfair to those of us who have been sectioned against our will. We are just ordinary people with a mental illness, who as a result of that illness lose insight into our own condition. I no longer wanted to be treated in hospital, I didn't feel that treatment was helping me, but the doctors wished to keep me safe, hence the conflict of interest which led to me being sectioned.

I once heard a friend in conversation say, 'it's not as if you have to be strapped down like a nutter'. Actually no one gets strapped down any longer in psychiatric hospitals in the UK, though I believe it still occurs in the more barbaric treatment of mental health patients in some parts of the world. But the perception is still here. I don't think it would get talked about if you thought it could possibly happen to you. Does anyone ever stop and think that it could happen to them – not the strapping down, but the mental illness? Yes, it happens to ordinary people like you and me. I had no family history, no postnatal depression, nothing to suggest that I would suffer such an extreme illness, but I did. I wonder whether anyone could point me out now as someone 'abnormal'. Reassuringly my family and friends do not think so. In fact my husband has said I was the last person he thought would ever develop depression, but I did.

Can These be Symptoms?

We continued to live in Southampton when I was writing *Life after Darkness*. One day I visited my GP because I just couldn't sleep. This had been going on for some months and I was becoming more and more tired. I was working late shifts, early shifts and nights in A&E, so I wondered whether it was this that was disrupting my sleeping pattern. The GP was singularly unhelpful about it and asked me what I wanted him to do, so I left with a two week prescription for sleeping tablets that I didn't want to take. I was researching my medical notes for the book and, as a result, had to look at them whilst my previous psychiatric consultant, David Baldwin was present (part of the NHS stipulation to viewing your own notes). He was a lovely, caring doctor and both Phil and I had a lot of time for him. When informally talking to him, I mentioned that I wasn't sleeping and he started to ask questions. After a little while he said to me that he thought I was depressed again. I didn't feel low and said so, but he insisted that it accounted for the other symptoms he had elicited, rather like migraine without the headache. This all happened very gently and he arranged to see me in his clinic and I accepted his advice to start antidepressants again straight away.

Well how good God is! When I had so dramatically recovered from the first episode, I was totally convinced that I was healed and that it was for good. When Christians asked me what I would do if it returned, I used to feel quite annoyed and confidently retorted that it wouldn't, after all, I had been healed. But when pushed I said I would get down on my knees and pray. However the same question was asked by David Baldwin before I discharged myself from his care and also by Professor Matthews in Dundee when I was reviewed at one and two years after my operation, as part of the ongoing research which takes place in his unit. I was very honest with both these doctors as the horrors of what I had gone through were still very real. I said I would go to the nearest high building and jump off and I meant it, such was my fear. Both of them had not seemed surprised at my reaction, but had the same response 'just get in touch with us before you do that'. So when this revelation that I was suffering with depression came, it was not nearly as bad as I could ever have anticipated and Dr Baldwin was quick to reassure me that it would be quickly brought under control with treatment. I accepted this. There was no need to jump off a building, although it did cause me to get down on my knees and pray!

Actually I had done a dreadful thing. Apart from my healthy desire not to suffer with this condition ever again, I had also become arrogant. I thought that I was not like other people who suffer recurrences of their depression, I was different, I had made it, I had suffered a major mental illness but I had recovered, I was healed. I think I had even put some of the stigma I so hated onto myself, believing: 'you aren't going to find me back with those sorts of problems anymore – I am sorted out'. I wrote in the book that I had suffered from a few weeks of mild depression because that's what seemed to happen; once I was back on antidepressants, my sleep improved and I regained my energy and lack of drive and the writing started back in earnest.

There is also another aspect to this; it is not for another to judge the sufferer who is suicidal, much of it is born out of the illness itself. It is the culmination of despair and desperation, but also suicidal thoughts are a symptom of the illness. I used to think of myself as so bad and rotten that I didn't deserve to live. But the cold hearted decision to throw myself off a building while I was well, rather than go through the trauma of another depression, was in fact a failure to trust God in all circumstances. In other words, it was sin and it needed to be dealt with as such. My recognition of this didn't happen immediately, in fact it was some years before I realised this and could confess that I had sinned, but God is infinitely patient and was waiting there with his forgiveness through Jesus.

However if someone is currently suicidal, it is likely to be generated by their illness and it would not do to try and confront them over this or other negative thoughts which are genuinely being felt and believed as true. They need to be listened to and ultimately what they need is medical or psychological help. If there is any indication that suicide is intended soon, then this is an emergency and they should be seen by a doctor without delay. God does not condemn them and neither should I. I think of the woman caught in adultery (John 8:1–11), those who initially wanted to stone her left one by one as they realised their own sin and Jesus did not condemn her. The reason I needed to come to God particularly in this situation was that I was well, but my heart did not trust the Lord.

I thought the depression was all over when I handed the manuscript to the publisher, but within a short time I started to feel bad again – only this time the lowness of mood was very much a feature. I continued to see Dr Baldwin and he referred me for CBT.

However unlike the first episode of depression, I continued working and was able to carry on with normal life and living; this was just mild depression – or so I thought.

The Prospect of a Move

In the summer of that year, 2005, Phil was made redundant and the only compensation was three months salary. He began looking for similar IT work in our area without any success. It was as though my fears were realised, because the future became so uncertain. I was earning well part time, but it was not enough to pay all the bills now we had our children's higher education to support. I had tried working full time at my job but found that the strain was too much. We began to realise that we might have to move and started seeking the Lord in earnest about our future. We felt God saying to us that we should move to Scotland; it was such a positive place for us, it was there that I had been released from depression, we had spent happy holidays there early in our marriage and my ancestry was Scottish. We needed to sell our house as we could no longer afford the mortgage and realised that we could scale down since the children were that bit older and were leaving home. The children were happy with our idea and Jonathan, though only 17, was keen to stay behind in Southampton and share a flat with his older brother. God also repeatedly confirmed that this was the right decision, so, despite the mild depression and the obvious disappointment that came with this news of the redundancy, we were by now excited at the prospect of doing something entirely new.

Unfortunately after a couple of months the depression was once again affecting my spiritual life. My prayer diary from that time records time and time again that I was fearful – not, as you would imagine, about the depression, but more about problems of everyday living.

I wrote this on 16 October 2005: 'Please forgive me for not seeking you, for straying from your pathway and giving in to fear. Fear is not from you, except godly fear. I know I am accountable to you – may only that fear be part of me.'

And again 10 days later:

Lord I lay down my fears. I surrender them to You. Your perfect love casts out fear. It has no place in my life, except that I may fear You when I know that You know everything I think and I will have to give an account to You. Right now I name these fears

- *fear of lack of time*
- *fear of lack of money*
- *fear of Phil being unhappy*
- *fear of the children being unhappy*
- *fear of *** (name of one of the consultants at work)*

The truth is You have promised to provide all I need. The truth is You care about Phil and the children more than I do. The truth is that their happiness and contentment is not my responsibility.

I did not lack time, although money had become an issue and there was no reason to think that Phil or the children were going to be unhappy, so my irrational fears were very much alive.

And on 18 November 2005:

What is my sin that so easily entangles me and that I need to lay aside?' (Heb 12:1–3). Fear. I am commanded not to be afraid, God's perfect love casts out fear. But fear is a strong driving force in my life. I am afraid of

- *tiredness*
- *finance*
- *making wrong decisions*
- *being sued*
- *what people think of me*
- *being exposed when I write*

Lord You are God and You made the universe and everything in it. You have promised to provide. You have said that if I

*pursue wisdom I will not stumble and if I understand Jesus'
love I will not stumble. You also pick me up when I fall down.
You have forgiven me and I am righteous only because of
Jesus. I need only fear one person and that is You God. What
You think of me is what matters. Holy Spirit come into me
and   strengthen   me   and   give
me Your wisdom and teach me to love others, because You
love me.*

And so it went on. What I meant by fearing God is not to do
with anxiety or being afraid, but rather an awesome, reverent
fear for He is almighty, all powerful and has our eternal
destiny in His hands, yet He is also filled with loving
kindness, slow to anger, forgiving, compassionate and our
Father.

Finally Phil was offered a job in Aberdeen, working in the
IT department of the Aberdeen Royal Infirmary. I was offered
a transfer to the A&E department at the same hospital;
everything was falling into place. But then I found out that I
would have to work almost double the hours than I had been
working down south, (yes, the part time hours would be 39
per week) and I would have to work seven night shifts
consecutively. In addition to this I would be sent on a
prolonged secondment to a hospital 100 miles away. Knowing
that I was vulnerable with mild depression, I turned this down
for the above reasons, but not before I saw an alternative.
There was a post in Psychiatry advertised and I could hardly
believe it when I was appointed to work as a staff grade
psychiatrist at the Royal Cornhill Hospital, right next door to
the Royal Infirmary. I was excited at this opportunity to 'put
something back' into the speciality that had cared so well for
me, but also at the prospect of doing normal working hours
with no on call, no shifts and no weekends.

6: Time in Hospital

When *Life after Darkness* was published I received nationwide publicity even though I had just moved. About two months later I had the enormous privilege of being asked to appear on GMTV, on *The Lorraine Kelly Show*. A fellow doctor came up to me at my new place of work; she called me over and whispered in my ear that she had read an article about the book in one of the medical journals. I was rather surprised at her whispering and said out loud that she could talk in a normal voice; my story was by then in the public domain and the staff and patients all knew about it having watched the programme on TV. My photo had been spread across the page of more than one newspaper. She apologised and said that she was not sure if I wanted people to know about it! We were working in a mental hospital amongst psychiatric patients and she questioned whether or not I wanted people to know about my past. In retrospect I am sure she had my best interests at heart. But the patients loved the fact that I had been treated for depression myself. I only ever came across one patient who tried to use it against me. Many more opened up to me and I really enjoyed looking after them. Not all the staff were always supportive though. I became upset because I felt a patient with depression was being treated unfairly and one of the nurses said to me 'you know your trouble, you're wet behind the ears'.

Our move had gone very smoothly all things considered and we rented a flat out of town and soon settled down into a church in Banchory, a small town about 20 miles from Aberdeen and made friends. We had not known anyone when we moved but how wonderful it is to find a readymade 'family' in the church. I didn't advertise the fact that I was suffering with depression and few people were aware of my past, particularly because they did not know me when the publicity for *Life after Darkness* had come out. I was busy at work but in the meantime my health started to deteriorate. I was once again referred for CBT, but this time the therapist felt that as I had just completed a course it would not be helpful to repeat it. I was assigned a CPN (community psychiatric nurse) too, who used to see me 'secretly' in my lunch hour. She would tell me which room she would be in and I would go to the room at a specified time, so I would not be seen in any waiting area. I began to wonder whether I had made the right choice to leave A&E, as being depressed and working as a psychiatrist seemed too close to the bone.

I looked into the possibility of returning to work in A&E but the doctor whom I saw to discuss this had come to find out about my current bout of depression. To cut a long story short, he told me how annoyed he and his colleagues had been at me turning down the specialist registrar post in his department and he was not in the least bit sympathetic towards me being depressed again. So the door was firmly closed.

The psychiatrist I was under in Aberdeen was very understanding but totally convinced that whatever happened I should continue working and that I would get over this slight relapse. But as time went on I grew worse; the fears were even more evident as was the accompanying anxiety. I was able to work competently putting on a front so that no one could guess what was going on inside, but, whenever I could, I would lock the door of my office and put chairs together to have a lie down and a cry. Soon I realised that my depression was becoming worse than many of the patients on the ward and it took all my energy to cover up the illness and function for all my duties. Finally I could not carry on at work any longer and took myself off sick.

About a week later I was once again highly suicidal so I visited my GP. I knew the consequence of this would be an admission to hospital, but I was even prepared to undergo that. Although I was suicidal I knew deep down that I didn't want to die, I just wanted an end to the tortured existence. My days were so long it seemed as if time stood still; the deep darkness had returned. I had no energy and could no longer cope with the household tasks which before I had undertaken without a thought. I stayed in bed all day while Phil was at work and my dark and dismal thoughts took over my life. I did pray, but God seemed very distant. I could not be admitted to my own hospital since I worked there, so it was arranged for me to go back to Dundee under the care of Professor Matthews again.

I had kept my illness as hidden as possible from my family; of course they were all back in England, so they were shocked at the news that I was going into hospital again, but I gave them the optimistic view that this would be just a short admission, as that is what I hoped for. Although this cover up had been motivated by not wanting to worry them, I understood after it was all over that, in fact, it had caused them even more alarm by seemingly coming out of the blue. How little I had learned.

Life in Dundee

Once at the Carseview Centre in Dundee (the psychiatric unit), I was distraught. I felt as though I had let the world down. Here I was the 'star patient', who had written a book describing my amazing recovery, who had articles written in the major newspapers about me, who had been on the radio and on television. I had failed. I was back to square one. I hit the lowest of the low. Once again I gave into the deep, dark thoughts that entered my mind. I was nothing, nobody but a miserable liar, deceiving everyone. I had no right to exist. I was surrounded by a black mist that clung like a cobweb to every part of me. I stopped eating and hardly drank at all, I longed to die. I wished I had cancer or some serious illness which would give my death legitimacy. I fell for the thoughts that were telling me that I was not ill, just bad, and that I was a complete fraud for being in the hospital.

Though I had my Bible with me, I couldn't read it; all I did was lie in bed all day wishing for the end. I don't remember praying. I don't remember telling myself all the truths; that the Father loved me, that I was a forgiven and redeemed child of God. All of these I had lived by every day during the previous five years of wellness. I simply had no energy left to remind myself of any of those things. It seemed that as my mental health deteriorated, so my spiritual health deteriorated and not the other way round (which is what some Christians assume).

However God had not left me; even though I felt nowhere near His presence I still had knowledge that He was there beside me. Indeed He was looking after me. Prof Matthews, a most kind and compassionate man, who by now had known me both when I had been seriously ill before the operation and when seriously well for the years afterwards, convinced me that I needed ECT. I was concerned about the memory loss, a side effect which can be experienced after ECT, but he assured me that they would do all they can to give me as few treatments as possible to get me better. He also reassured me that I would get better. I know I was very much afraid, despite the advice; I thought that once again I was going to be in the hospital for years and years, but it was my lack of intake that was by now causing problems and the blood tests showed that I had the early signs of my kidneys starting to fail. ECT was once again vitally necessary in order to get me well enough to eat and drink.

Reassuringly the experience of ECT was much better than I had known it to be before. It took place in a purpose built room, with resuscitation equipment highly visible. Professor Matthews was there to oversee it, and he was a very comforting presence; a consultant had never been there during the ECT back in the DOP at Southampton. After a very few treatments I started to respond and slowly my appetite returned. They had rehydrated me while I was under anaesthetic, but then I started to drink. The deep depression lifted and I was able to get out of bed and start socialising with other patients on the ward. Professor Matthews had always been reassuring and kept on telling me that since I had had the surgery the relapse I was suffering would now be amenable to treatment. He was absolutely right, but it took time. My faith in God returned fully but I remained 'deluded' by depressive thinking. Prof used to write down what he had said for me in my notebook that I used as a diary, so I could remind myself when he was not there. I was in need of constant reassurance, because my thoughts were so self punitive and also because severe depression affects your memory. This is what he wrote for me on 31 January 2007:

1) *The team are **not** cross with you.*

2) *The team believe that you are unwell – specifically depressed. Sometimes you lose the ability to see this. We have no doubts about this!*

3) *We do **not** believe that you are bad. You are **not** wasting our time.*

4) *Presently – the team believe that you need to be treated in hospital. You would not be safe at home.*

5) *The restrictions on your 'freedom' are in place to try to help to keep you safe.*

*6)   I have suggested that we do not change medication (or dose) today to see if the nausea might settle. We **will** change that if it does not.*
7)   Bob is planning to see you on Friday.

I would look forward to his visits and God truly encouraged me through them and the wisdom that he used in giving me ECT and getting me onto the right drug treatment. I also had contact with his clinical nurse specialist, Bob MacVicar who at a later date started psychotherapy with me; like the Prof he is in my mind one of those truly great people, immensely kind and unusually understanding. Both of them are dedicated to their jobs of caring for those with serious mental health problems, treating each patient as an individual, giving us hope and maintaining our self respect. Unlike the psychotherapy I had experienced in Southampton, Bob did not root around in my past, rather he gave me tools by which I could tackle my false perceptions and depressive thinking myself. The depressed mentally ill often seem to be self indulgent. I know I was selfish, locked in and isolated by my thinking which made me feel that physically I was on my own. Of course this was not true and I was lucky I had Phil. But one of the reasons it is so necessary to have professional input is that when I shared my thoughts, it would make Phil feel helpless and my longing was that he would not be in pain for me. It was more important that we could stand strong together rather than inadvertently bring one another down.

A New Experience

Another amazing thing started happening at this time. My new church started writing to me, sending cards and presents. I was sent flowers from my family and talked to them on my mobile phone. All these things, including Phil's visits, said I was loved, even though I thought I was unbearable and unlovable. But it was all so important in reinforcing the message that the medical team were giving me: 'You are not bad, you are ill'. I was in a single room which gave me privacy and eventually I started to read the Bible again. I had cards from members of the church I barely knew and the minister visited me, despite the hospital being 60 miles away from home. As time went on, and I improved, I was allowed out for some weekends; a lady from church, Christine, who I hardly knew started to help Phil out with the drives to Dundee and would come and fetch me.

Once again it was hard for Phil; the round trip to visit me would take three hours, but he faithfully visited me at least twice a week.

I was overwhelmed by the church's love and support. It was wonderful. At last I felt that here was a group of Christians who knew no stigma. Even though I was an inpatient for six months, the cards did not stop coming. Sometimes I was afraid to go to church during the weekends that I was 'on leave' from hospital, despite the fact that I was accepted just as I was, without judgement or having to undergo extensive scrutiny. I found the energy of meeting people and the effort I had to make to face them just too much. (This may happen for much milder degrees of mental illness and it is good to remember that for a sufferer to come to church on Sunday may be quite an ordeal for them and it may well have taken a great deal of courage.)

Life on Ward 1

As in any hospital ward there was a certain routine to the day, but that is where the similarity ended. I really did appreciate the fact that, most of the time, we had our own rooms at the Carseview Centre, which afforded the much sought after privacy that we needed. It was built so there were two corridors, one which contained rooms for women and the other for men. The ward was carpeted, which was really nice too, except for when it came to cleaning. Since 2001, when I had been there for surgery, the whole place was no longer new and how quickly it seemed the ward had deteriorated physically. The first room I was in on my own was smelly – a previous occupant must have been incontinent and the cleaner did her best for me by coming in daily and spraying it with deodorising spray, but unhappily this didn't really do the trick. Then for some reason for which I cannot remember, the male and female corridors changed. This meant a room change and I was on the garden side of the corridor so was able to look out into the courtyard garden, which was good.

I slept much better now because of the medication, but that also meant that I found I needed more than just a night's sleep. The morning wake up call was just that; the nurses went down the corridors knocking on each door with the shout of 'breakfast' or 'medication', I can't remember which. I used to dress over my pyjamas because you were not allowed to wear night clothes outside of your room. I was supposed to have the pills before breakfast and all I wanted was a bowl of cereal as I longed to go back to sleep. Sometimes the wait was long for the nurses to actually come and start dishing them out. Medication queues were not the place for social interaction and there were no chairs, so it was not easy for the likes of tired me.

After breakfast I would go back to bed and have my shower in the en-suite shower room later – the en-suite was another vast improvement on what I had come across before in mental hospitals. I was often woken again with the shout of coffee and that meant queuing up again to be served our hot drink in a plastic mug. All the crockery was plastic, I assume someone in 'health and safety' had decided that breakables on a psychiatric ward were not suitable, though the brightly coloured cups for water did give me a bit of a feeling that not much thought had gone into it. I couldn't help feeling like I was back at school both then and in the dining room and the staff were the matrons, especially as there was always a nurse standing watching over the situation. If only they would sit down with us...but then they had their own coffee breaks, their 'time out'.

It wouldn't be that long before lunch, all the mealtimes were early in the day and it was hard to bear the times in between the meals and coffee breaks. I would sit with patients in the dining room, sometimes just where there was an empty place – particularly if it was someone I had befriended or if I was feeling bad, I might try and get a place on my own. One lady had a particular place she would sit and 'owned it' – she got so mad if anyone else sat on that table, so we let her be. All newcomers had to be warned not to sit there, including me when I first started using the dining room. The queues became very much a part of life, ten times a day for meals, drinks and medication. The worst time though was before bed. I usually wanted to get to bed early, but had to wait until 10pm for medication. I wanted to be near the start of the queue as practically everyone had night time meds, so it could take some time. So I would often go early before the call for medication. Then it was on to the queue for night time milky drinks...if I wasn't careful, I would find the sedative effect of the medication had started to take effect before I was actually in bed and I would find myself holding on to the furnishings as I felt so sedated yet needed to clean my teeth and get undressed, until I could finally go to sleep.

I found myself feeling really tired such a lot that I just wanted to lie down, but when I was more awake it was difficult to know what to do. As I improved I would try and read the Bible, but my concentration was poor. However for some reason, I don't know why, I became interested in Sudoku and that led on to 'killer Sudoku', which was much more challenging. The great thing was that while I was doing the puzzle I did not think about anything else; it completely took over all my thought processes which gave me a rest from the depression. So I tried to do at least one puzzle a day – there were puzzle books sold in the shops at the main hospital, so it was easy enough to get hold of them. I believe God gave this to me as rest and relaxation, it really helped as I could not read and I found it really hard in the day room. There was a small day room for women only and sometimes there were interesting programmes to watch on TV, although the more dominant figures tended to dictate what was on. I felt so uncomfortable when disputes arose over what programme to watch and sometimes the nurses would intervene. For the most part I just put up with it and was forced to watch programmes I wouldn't choose, but, happily for me, the TV wasn't on all the time, and it was another place to be other than my room and those of us who used it developed a certain camaraderie.

One thing I found distressing was when one of the women became ill, physically. Her room was opposite mine and we were right at the end of the corridor. She was a smoker and developed an awful chest infection. The trouble was she just wasn't receiving the attention she needed for her illness. Her breathing kept me awake at night as with my medically trained powers of observation listening, not only to her but also to what the nurses were saying, made me realise she was seriously ill. Finally I got up in the night and summoned the nursing staff once again to say that she needed a doctor, not in the morning, but now! I was so relieved when the ambulance arrived and removed her the 500 yards or so to the A&E department and she was admitted to the general hospital. It made me very uneasy though that I had had to instigate it, but the mental health nurses are not trained in physical medicine, so it's not a good place to be ill.

I remember periods when I became quite agitated – the thoughts would become overwhelming and I realised that at times like that I just needed to talk. But it did not always happen at a convenient time for the staff. It was great if you could be 'given time', but this was often postponed, so I would be offered lorazepam (a tranquiliser) as an alternative, or perhaps a suggestion would be made to do my Sudoku or listen to music. Sometimes a nursing assistant would come and talk to me or take me round the block for a walk. The latter was preferable because these women were not trained and often I felt talked down to. Somehow the system was such that the trained staff did not have much time with their patients, I suppose paperwork as usual made sure of that. There were inevitably some staff who I took to more than others and my key nurse was one of them. She was very kind and did attempt to find time to spend with me.

While I was eating in the dining room, at my eye level, there was a poster which I thought would have been more appropriately pinned up in the staff office or coffee room. It was telling staff to respect patients, which I found a little difficult to understand, if only because it didn't seem to make the slightest difference. Most of the qualified nurses and nursing assistants were kind and understanding, respectful too, but those who were not...I don't think it occurred to them that the posters were aimed at them. We patients tended to suffer in silence. It soon became clear who to avoid and for the most part I tried to stay clear of the minority of staff who were bullies.

The food was all precooked and packaged and needed to be reheated in special ovens, so there was no such thing as fresh vegetables. The staff and patients alike were astounded that these meals reached us by road, driven all the way from a plant in the north of England. I was not eating well and I desperately craved a salad; there were kitchens on the Ninewells site, in fact the rest of the hospital was fed from these kitchens, but to have a salad was to demand special treatment. I was referred to the dietician and I explained my desire for something fresh. Fortunately she realised that I needed to eat something and at least a salad was healthy for one meal a day. Along with this I was also given nutritional drinks to build me up, such was the absurdity of the situation.

Difficult Times

What I really hated was when I had the misfortune to be placed under close observation, which was felt necessary on several occasions for me since I was suicidal and had once again started to harm myself. I wasn't confined to my room, but I had to be accompanied by a nurse – of course the qualified staff members were too busy to be involved in such duties for any length of time and a rota was set up mostly consisting of nursing assistants. When I was in my room, two of them had to sit outside the door. Apparently once a patient had walked up the corridor when a single nurse was sitting outside a door and had pulled her pony tail, so now two nurses were assigned so they could protect each other. The trouble was that they were bored. They didn't talk to me, the patient, but they talked to each other; the door to my room had fortified glass windows in it and these were not enough to drown out noise. It was awful, often I wanted to rest and sleep but I was kept awake by the chatter. It went on through the night as it did when others were on close observation and so most of us in the corridor were kept awake. I was amazed that they simply didn't mind us all hearing the conversation, but it was the laughter during peace and quiet that was the worst. I did pluck up courage to ask them to be quiet during the night and often they would oblige but only for a few minutes as soon they would forget and the volume would creep up again; it could be impossible to get any sleep. I remember one night when one of my fellow patients lost her cool and told them in no uncertain terms to be quiet. Unfortunately she was told not to shout, by someone who was shouting at her! When I brought this to the attention of one of the senior nurses, she admitted that they were noisy, but I was told to consider the 'poor night nurses' – this was their daytime! Why they couldn't change turns more frequently and be given the instruction to read or whisper quietly I do not know.

There was a particular woman on the night staff, a nursing assistant who was nearing her retirement, who refused to sit on the hospital chairs without a towel beneath her, despite the fact that she was in uniform. The chairs which patients sat on were too dirty for her; it used to make me feel angry – we had to sit on them, so why shouldn't she. She never had a sympathetic word for anyone, appeared heartless and certainly did not treat us with respect. I remember being told off for having my mobile phone outside my room, but later that day I recorded in my diary she was walking down the corridor speaking into hers. It was very hard to take. I certainly had to harness God's grace.

But a rather worse situation came to pass. On this occasion I was on close observation and she was one of the two nursing assistants sitting outside the room door. I needed to visit the toilet and went into the bathroom. She jumped up and opened the bathroom door – I explained that I needed privacy, as I was constipated and asked to be left alone. I had had toilet privacy from the other staff that day and I had not self harmed. She refused and a confrontation ensued, but she was adamant that she was not going to let me go into the bathroom on my own despite my protests and promises that I would be safe. I wanted her to call a staff nurse but she refused that, so I made to go out of my room to find one, which I was perfectly entitled to do as I wasn't confined to my room. In response she and the other nursing assistant barricaded the door, effectively holding me prisoner. I became profoundly upset and started crying. I became angry and, though I was sobbing, I shouted at her and so eventually she called for a staff nurse. The staff nurse who came sat on the bed beside me with her arm around me and gently asked what the problem was. I told her and she allowed me to visit the bathroom privately. However I was left shaken and unhappy. A few days later I apologised to this nurse for shouting at her, but she never said a word in return! It was really hard to maintain a forgiving attitude.

This is not supposed to be a particular criticism of this hospital, or of nursing assistants in general, rather an indictment of the system that denies patients' access to nurses fully trained in mental health to actually nurse them while in hospital. Surely this is what they are trained for, yet UK wide you hear the same story; that the nurses have not got enough time to spend with their patients.

Further Therapies

The occupational therapy time on the ward had been cut, which meant that the one part time occupational therapist was only able to spend half a day on the ward. She used to run a meeting for us with the incentive of chocolate biscuits! For goodness sake, this really felt like being a child at school! During this time, we were able to tell her of our life on the ward and she promised to pass on our grievances, but nothing changed.

I had time to observe much that went on during my stay. I had to accept the cleaning standards even though they weren't as high as mine at home. The cleaners were lovely ladies, but they had to work with the set up which was given to them.

They had a trolley with their cleaning equipment on, which included a bucket. In this bucket was kept a toilet cleaning brush and various cloths hung on the side of the bucket. The cloth which was used for wiping the toilet seat and surrounds was kept right next to the same cloth which was used to wipe around the basin and taps. There was nothing to keep the toilet brush from dripping on either of them. It used to make me shudder when I cleaned my teeth and I didn't want to put my toothbrush down on the sink. The cleaner wore a pair of plastic gloves and these were not changed whatever job she was doing or between patient rooms. I didn't feel it was fair to criticise the individual cleaners for this – they were only doing what they had been taught to do, so I described the situation to the nursing staff. They were sympathetic but explained that they had nothing to do with it – this was the housekeeping department's territory. When I was getting better, I tried to see the head of housekeeping for the unit, but, despite this being taken up by the helpful occupational therapist, I was never able to see anyone. Around Christmas a vomiting virus came to the ward and not surprisingly it spread rapidly from patient to patient – I don't think the lack of hygiene around the cleaning of bathrooms had helped, but I became obsessive about cleaning the handles to my room door and the bathroom door as well as washing my hands vigorously before meals. Praise God, He kept me safe and I was one of the exceptions – I didn't catch the bug!

Most patients were allowed out and about and the views of the Tay estuary on the walk around the building were stunning. But, for a lot of my time, I had to be escorted by a member of staff as it wasn't felt that I was well enough to go out on my own. This meant my time outside in the fresh air was very restricted as the staff were so busy. When I used to sit and look out of my window, I found myself so aware of the rubbish which had gathered around the shrubs and flowerbeds of the gardens, so, in the spring time, I requested that I be allowed out to gather it up. I really enjoyed myself in the garden and felt so satisfied that it was a more pleasant place for all of us, especially knowing that cleaning up was something which probably wouldn't otherwise be done until the grounds men appeared in the summer.

When I was well on my way to getting better, I found out about the gym. You had to be referred by the doctor and my request to attend was successful. I was able to go for half an hour twice a week, the maximum time allowed as there weren't enough physiotherapy staff to supervise it. I had never attended a gym before and they had about six pieces of equipment that we could take turns in using. I really found it helpful and was just sad that I couldn't access it more often. I wondered why, when these new premises had been built especially for psychiatric patients, there was not enough money to adequately staff them. I know from others that my experience is by no means unique.

Government statistics consistently show that mental health problems are the greatest contributors to the nation's sickness record, but it is not a 'popular', high profile speciality like cancer or heart disease. I have the greatest sympathy for anyone who has the misfortune to suffer from any of these diseases and have absolutely nothing against them receiving the appropriate amount of funding, but mental health does not get its fair share. Despite some improvement in funding, it remains a 'Cinderella' speciality. The stigma that is attached to psychiatric illness is also attached to those who work in the speciality. Doctors, often nicknamed 'shrinks' are not seen as 'proper' doctors and many vacancies for psychiatric posts remain unfilled; the same is true to a lesser extent with psychiatric nurses. The lack of understanding of what a psychiatrist does amongst the medical profession is astonishing. I heard recently of a senior, academic specialist in medicine who still thought a psychiatrist used a couch! Shame on you medical profession. Why are you not honouring those who dedicate their lives to psychiatric medicine in the way you would someone who is practicing as a surgeon? Depression, schizophrenia, bipolar disorder and personality disorders are all causes of premature death, as well as other mental health illnesses, so why are they not seen as priorities?

We do Need Prayer

In the Church, we are always very concerned for friends who suffer from cancer, heart disease or stroke; but who can blame us for being just as blind to the suffering caused by other disorders than any of the general public? However we all know of someone suffering from a mental illness. I was so grateful that there had been the urgency of the prayer and the collective concern surrounding my illness.

I know there are different degrees of mental illness. Take depression for example. I do not typify a common case as I have suffered at the extreme end of the spectrum of seriousness and the term depression is often used by the lay person for describing normal sadness. But the general public are being informed of mental health disorders and the very real suffering they cause, so it is good that we the Church are being informed and are ready to look after those who become extremely vulnerable while suffering from such conditions. Yet though I have been in the position of needing help myself, I rejoice that there will be many people like me who recover and can then go on to minister and empathise with others who are 'going through the mill'.

7: Changes from Home

Professor Matthews discharged me home in April 2007. My admission had lasted six months but he continued to see me regularly as an outpatient as I wasn't fully well when I was discharged, though certainly on the way, and well enough to be at home. I also had sessions arranged for psychotherapy with Bob, also part of the team. As I have said he is a lovely man, who is empathic, kind and full of wisdom. I do believe that God works through men like these even though they are not believers. Both of them knew Phil and had done a good job of keeping him informed and in the picture while I was in hospital. They always asked after him if he did not happen to accompany me to appointments. The fact that it was over an hour's drive from Banchory to get to Dundee was no deterrent as I found the visits so helpful.

It is a well known fact in psychiatry that the first two weeks after discharge can be a very difficult, sometimes dangerous, time for the patient, as he or she adjusts to life outside the confines and the shelter of an institution. But I was tremendously happy to be at home and had had ample preparation through longer and longer leave periods there before I was discharged.

It was of course much easier for Phil, as now he didn't have to visit me and also I was able to take over many aspects of the housekeeping straightaway. The one task which I found hardest to do, and do even now, was the cooking of the evening meal. I don't know why, but I dreaded it and found simple things like peeling potatoes took a major effort. For a while Phil did this just as soon as he arrived home from work.

However, before too long, I was back at the helm once more, as far as the housekeeping was concerned.

Out and About

It took some courage to start socialising and I had never just been 'at home' in Banchory before, as I had been working previously. But I soon joined one of the local ladies' Bible study groups from our church and I also found a keep fit class at the local school. I was well able to put on a good face to do these activities, even though I was still recovering and my mood carried on fluctuating to some degree; I hadn't reached anything like normal yet. I was settling in with my new group of friends and getting to know some of the givers of the lovely cards and gifts I had been sent while I was in hospital. There were far more women 'at home' than I would have found to be the case in Southampton despite the fact that many had children the same age as ours who were at university or other places of education. This immediately gave me something in common with my new friends, even though I was always aware that our children had grown up elsewhere. Even though I did not have the history of relationship that many of these friends had with each other, I was always made to feel welcome and not treated as a 'newcomer'.

Putting on my 'good face' comes naturally to me when I feel down. I have tried to analyse it and wonder whether I am being dishonest. However if people who are in pain don't complain or show it they are admired, and I had no desire to burden others with how I might be feeling. Especially when I am not so ill, I can honestly put my emotions aside for the duration of the social activity that I am encountering and I am sure it does me good. I also have no desire for people to feel sorry for me or take pity on me. Anyway, during that time I would rather not have been seen as someone who was ill by friends who barely knew me – after all, they knew I had recently been discharged from hospital and that was enough.

Clan Gathering

That summer all our children came up to visit us at some point so it was a busy time, but the most significant time for me was going to 'Clan Gathering', a Scottish version of 'New Wine'. This was a conference for Christians from all over Scotland who came together at a site near St Andrew's to worship and hear various Christian speakers, some of whom were international. We stayed with some friends called Andrew and Valerie whom we had met when we were first thinking of moving to Scotland and they were very hospitable towards us. I was able to go to meetings at Clan as I felt able, but at other times I just relaxed in their lovely home and garden.

Two keynote speakers I heard were to stand out for me in particular. One was R.T. Kendall and his inspirational talk on 'forgiveness' and the other was Mark Stibbe. Mark spoke on the fatherhood of God and what I most clearly remember I personalised. It was from him that I first heard about the fact that God was not just 'God the Father', but God, my Father, my Abba, my Dad. It had a profound impact on me; you see I always knew my earthly father loved me, he played games with me in the garden when I was young, he and my mother taught me how to express myself verbally, he taught me a sense of duty, but he is a child of his time and didn't show much affection. I had never heard him say to me 'I love you' which we so frequently said to our children and to each other. (We never make the same mistakes as our parents!) Both my parents showed us what I think was a 'conditional' love, that is we earned their approval with good manners, doing well at school, liking the sorts of things they liked and I was very conformist wishing to please them as best I could. I had held this against them at one time but had since forgiven them and realised that it was in no way personal to me – it was just as a result of their own upbringing. When I was at boarding school a letter from my father was rare but on the few occasions that he wrote, he would always sign himself as 'your affectionate Pa' and I treasured those letters. But, because of these things, I had unwittingly projected my earthly father's attributes onto God my Father. I could say all the right things, like 'God loves me', but I had never really *felt* His love or His pleasure. I had symptoms of an 'orphan heart', which was the main theme of Mark Stibbe's message. He taught how we are adopted into the family of God. I quote from his book *From Orphans to Heirs*:

God has been revealing his 'electing' or better still, his 'adopting grace'. God has been revealing himself as the Abba who adopts children into the everlasting embrace of the Godhead. This is the image of God which we so desperately need to have revealed to us today. As we allow the Holy Spirit to testify to our spirits that we are children of God, and as we form our understanding of God from the fatherly qualities described in scripture, then we will be released from slavery into sonship. We will be truly liberated to worship the Father in spirit and in truth.

I had somehow missed out on this revelation of God as my Father, so I went forward for prayer for healing of the 'orphan heart' condition, but nothing dramatic seemed to happen. However I was greatly encouraged by hearing testimonies of how other Christians there were released and changed.

I definitely needed a touch from God. The worship was so uplifting and as the days at the conference shot by, I felt more and more free and my remaining low mood lifted. I believe that Mark's word started a process in me whereby I gradually learnt to meet God the Father as my Abba, but not quite yet as my Daddy. Jesus called the Father 'Abba', which in His day was the equivalent for Papa, so I knew Daddy was not an irreverent word, but rather an admission that we really are His children and His love for us is boundless and immeasurable. I took great comfort in imagining myself sitting on Abba's knee with His loving arms around me, something I had seen with my children and their own father, but had no memory of as a child. I quote Mark Stibbe again, this time from his book entitled *The Father You've Been Waiting For*:

But God is a loving Father – the most loving Father in the universe. Wherever you are on your spiritual journey, his desire is that you come home and experience his affectionate embrace. He wants you to know that his is not like many earthly fathers, that he is always there for you and that you can trust him 100 per cent.

When I returned to outpatients after that holiday, I was feeling much better. I put it down to God and the visit to 'Clan', but the Prof thought it was because I had just had an increase in the dose of my antidepressant. However it was Bob who reminded me at a later date that it was after Clan that I really seemed to come out of the depths.

Inner Turmoils

I used to batter myself about the head over my lack of boldness in speaking out about 'God's healing', when in fact I should have known better. I am called *to be* a witness and that does not always necessitate speaking out. Prof and Bob knew that I attributed my healing to God's intervention and in fact I recognise that all recovery and healing comes from God anyway! So whether it was the pills or the Clan visit I don't know, perhaps a mixture of both, but I was feeling much lighter and a whole lot better.

But I still thought I was a lousy Christian and, in fact, I was in some ways. I carried unforgiveness in my heart. There were various situations and encounters I had had during my life, which left me with a grudge. Phil had bought two books by R.T. Kendall: *Total Forgiveness* and *Totally Forgiving Ourselves* and, since hearing the author at Clan, I was keen to read them when I arrived back home. As I read both these books, I was often stopped by the need for prayer and repentance as I realised how I had let bitterness into my heart. My heavenly Father and I had business to do and, by His grace, I was able to forgive the individuals involved and pray God's blessing on them; by this process of releasing them, I was also setting myself free. Here is a quote from *Total Forgiveness*:

> *We only hurt ourselves when we dwell on what has happened to us and fantasise about what it will be like when 'they' get punished. Most of all, we grieve the Holy Spirit of God. This is why we lose that inner peace.*

As I reread *Total Forgiveness* to write this passage, I was struck by what I had written about in the last chapter about the events at Carseview. I needed to challenge myself once again – had I really forgiven the nurses who barricaded me in my room? Why was I writing about it? As I examine myself, I can honestly say I have forgiven them and bear no ill feeling towards them, but I really do not want to minimise this sort of event. It happened to me and was just an example of a number of times when I seemed to come off worse after an incident in hospital. As with the noise at night, I didn't feel I wanted to make a formal complaint, I was scared that it might be counted against me.

When an inpatient in Southampton I wrote a letter of complaint, with the help of an advocacy service; the reply from the hospital management turned the event around and said it was my fault that a nurse became angry with me! I was very upset by this, but despite the help I had from my advocate I couldn't face going into battle over it, so I let it drop. The complaint is supposed to be kept separately from the medical notes and to my horror when researching for *Life after Darkness*, I found it lodged in them...now even more I am wary! (It has since been removed.) I am relatively articulate and know something of what's right. Unfortunately bad things do happen on psychiatric wards – I've heard enough stories from fellow patients, but they are tolerated by staff and patients alike. Needless to say there is plenty more I could say and patients are not entirely blameless. But I do think qualified mental health nurses are underpaid for the job they do, but this does not excuse the minority who have bad attitudes. (I would not want this to put people off making complaints – I was unfortunate that this one led to a bad outcome, but I think there is a better system and attitude towards making complaints now. I think letters of complaint and of encouragement are highly valuable.)

I digress. The other necessary spiritual principle that I desperately needed to learn and constantly have to practice is to forgive myself. Depression makes me blame, hate and judge myself and, even when I am feeling better, the tendency still remains. I quote R.T. Kendall once again, this time from *Totally Forgiving Ourselves*:

It is for this very reason that we are required to forgive ourselves – because God says so. How can it bless him, bring him honour and glory, when he forgives us but we don't forgive ourselves? It is like a slap in the face!

96

I also suffered from false guilt or pseudo guilt; Kendall explains: 'False guilt is a sense of shame in our hearts that God did not put there'. In other words, I felt guilty about all sorts of things that weren't my fault and for things which I wasn't responsible for, like my illness. When we suffer with guilt that the Holy Spirit brings it is rather the conviction of sin, and should lead to repentance; of course the Father is ready loving us and waiting to show us His forgiveness. So what with this and the revelation of God's Fatherhood, I had a lot of spiritual growing up and healing to be done.

I would like to say I found a mentor to help me through these things, but I did not have that privilege. For whatever reason, God has graciously allowed me to find out these spiritual truths through Christian literature and through the preaching at Clan. I am, though, very privileged to have a husband who can help me pray them into being. But unfortunately when my mood is low, depressive thinking returns once more. Kendall points out that emotional problems don't go away just because we have found faith in Christ. However for the future I am hoping that I am better equipped to fight those terrible, all encompassing thoughts.

My Position in the Sick Role

I continued to see Bob, but the bad news was that Prof Matthews had been diagnosed with a serious illness and needed treatment. I missed him as my doctor, but I realised that even when God provides us with such support, it is not good to become too dependent on it. So I wished him well and prayed for him, but was greatly relieved when he recovered and came back to work a few months later.

In the meantime I had to encounter another situation which caused me great anxiety. Ever since I had left hospital, I had struggled with a huge amount of guilt about being off sick, (false guilt!). I was in touch with the team I had worked for at Royal Cornhill Hospital and they assured me that my job was still open for me when I was ready to come back. I put myself under enormous pressure, seeing myself as lazy, a scrimper and a scrounger, a coward and a hypochondriac for the offence of being at home. Whenever I brought this up with Bob, he would point out to me that my mood had not stabilised, I was still having significant low periods and even the way I viewed my predicament wasn't a healthy one, so his advice was that I needed to be off work. In fact what I was not admitting to was that I was beating myself at home leaving painful bruises, which did not show beneath my clothing. I was not well. I saw Dr Christmas, another really good psychiatrist who was part of the team, while Prof was away and he was in agreement with Bob. It was too soon to be thinking about a return to work.

A while later I had to see the Occupational Health department at work and the physician there assessed me and was also of the opinion that I should remain off sick. He actually wondered whether the time would ever come that I could return to my current post. I remember being shocked at myself as I came to realise that maybe being a doctor on a psychiatry ward may not be the right path for me to take. Gradually peace came over me as, with Phil, I made the decision to accept medical retirement from my job. This did not mean I would never work again, but rather that I could not return to that particular post and a great weight was lifted from my mind.

This marked another step in improvement of my condition; I was gradually climbing up the hill to normality although it wasn't by a straight line – rather by an undulating one. I was very sensitive to the usual life events which take place along the way and, as I gradually improved, my thinking was returning back to normal.

The Privilege of Serving

Time moved on and, in the church, things were going well. Both Phil and I were very involved and we were felt really privileged to be asked to serve as elders. Our minister Donald came to tell us and explained the process within the Church of Scotland. Apparently once the existing elders had put forward the suggestion and the person or couple as in our case, have agreed, notice would be given to the church congregation so that they would have the ability to raise objections; but Donald reassured us that in his experience no one had ever objected, it was just a formality.

However he was about to learn to handle the exception that proves the rule. An objection came concerning me; someone in the congregation was concerned that my mental health problems could disqualify me from making important decisions regarding the church. So on the Sunday morning before the service that was going to instate us, an emergency meeting of the elders was called. Fortunately they overruled the objection and I did in fact become an elder. When I look back at this incident several things come to mind.

Firstly I feel absolutely no ill will towards the persons who made the objection. It was completely their right to do so. But secondly I do believe this came out of a stigmatising attitude. None of us can be sure that we will be in a fit state to make decisions all of the time, however discrimination against those who suffer with depression or other mental illnesses is actually against the law. If we were to stop people from carrying out their duties whether in employment or in the voluntary sector or in the church on such grounds, we would have to exclude 25 per cent of the population!

As an elder, I would not be making decisions in isolation and I would have the ability to step down whilst unwell or indisposed for any reason, so this was certainly a flawed objection. Fortunately I was able to see the funny side of this, but deep down I was disturbed that this had happened in our open, tolerant church.

Despite the tightening up of the law to include mental health problems in the Disabilities Discrimination Act, I have heard from other patients that they have been discriminated against but do not want to bring this to attention, as otherwise their illness would become public knowledge. In a sense we are our own worst enemies for as long as we are fearful of stigma, the law cannot help us to avoid it. It is therefore absolutely paramount that should such injustice be found in a church or Christian workplace, we must do our best to rectify it and I am so grateful that our church elders did so. I have to say that many sufferers, especially doctors, are very reluctant to let their colleagues or employers know about their illnesses; yet if everyone owned up, then we would soon see that mental health problems are so widespread, it would be much more difficult for any discrimination to occur. But God our Father is so good, His plans for us, as it says in Jeremiah 29:11, are to prosper us and not to harm us, to give us a hope and a future. So, if and when discrimination occurs, I know that I am well looked after. I am so thankful that Jesus paid the price for me.

8: Why Me?

Two men went up to the temple to pray, one a Pharisee and the other a tax collector. The Pharisee stood by himself and prayed: 'God I thank you that I am not like other people – robbers, evildoers, adulterers – or even like this tax collector. I fast twice a week and give a tenth of all I get.' But the tax collector stood at a distance. He would not even look up to heaven, but beat his breast and said, 'God have mercy on me, a sinner.' Luke 18:11–13

We know the end of this story that Jesus told, how the tax collector was justified rather than the Pharisee. This makes me think about who I might rather not be. What if I said I thank you God that I am not like this person with Schizophrenia, or this person with learning difficulties or this person with dementia? Sometimes our life circumstances humble us and sometimes unwittingly our health, wealth, race or profession causes us to be exalted in our own eyes. I might pray, asking God to stop me being proud, but I don't always like His answers. Even within the category of mental illness, there are some diagnoses that are more acceptable than others. When I wasn't getting better during the first episode of depression, some of the nurses labelled me as having a personality disorder and I was very upset. I used to think that when I was labelled in that way, I was somehow being blamed for my illness. Now it was alright for me to blame myself, but when the nurses who were there to help me agreed I felt so thoroughly rejected, it hurt more than anything else. I felt wretched. Fortunately only a minority of staff thought this way and none of my doctors did, so when I stop to think about it, I wonder what that was all about. Even when I worked as a psychiatrist the same sort of thing happened – if a patient with depression did not appear to be responding to treatment, the diagnosis of personality disorder would soon be considered, so I was obviously not unique in acquiring the label. It is disturbing because patients with a personality disorder are often felt wrongly to be beyond help and it has become a bit of a derogatory term amongst those who should know better.

One thing I have consistently heard is 'why me'? This applies to many circumstances. 'God's in control, so why does He let this happen?' or 'if there was a God, He wouldn't let this happen'.

One of the ladies I prayed for after I recovered, who had terminal cancer, was asking just these questions. She said it was easier for non-Christians because they didn't believe there was a God who heals, but she knew that God could heal her anytime, so was angry that He didn't choose to do so. Wonderfully she came to accept her situation before she died and passed away very much at peace with her Maker.

If anyone were to ask me the question 'why?' when I am depressed, the answer undoubtedly would be 'because I am a bad person', but now when I am well, I realise that is not any answer at all.

I am exploring a number of helpful possibilities, not because I need an answer – I don't. But rather, I would not like to miss this opportunity on my life's journey to take every advantage of learning more about what God wants to do with me. One thing I have learned is from Genesis 50, when Joseph addresses his brothers:

Don't be afraid. Am I in the place of God? You intended to harm me, but God intended it for good to accomplish what is now being done, the saving of many lives.

I believe the enemy intended to harm me, but God intended it for good. Some of my life's dreams are shattered; it has caused me so much pain thinking of what I missed with the children, when I wanted to be a first class mum, and in my relationship with my husband. Even though I went back to Emergency Medicine after my first bout of depression, I gave up on my training when we moved to Scotland. I may make it back to working in that field again, but if so it will be very part time and I will never make it to consultant.

Higher Purposes

God whispers to us in our pleasures, speaks to us in our conscience, but shouts in our pains: It is His megaphone to rouse a deaf world.
From *The Problem of Pain* by C.S. Lewis

God certainly did cause me to take Him more seriously, but that was in my miraculous healing rather than the illness itself. I take the point though; I want to hear God speak through my pain too. Then I came to hear about Larry Crabb and read some of his books. He doesn't have the all the answers either, in the end only God knows, but the Lord has spoken to me through some of his writing.

In his book *Shattered Dreams*, Larry Crabb says:

God's restraint has a purpose. When He appears to be doing nothing, He is doing something we've not yet learned to value and therefore cannot see. Only in the agony of His absence, both in the real absence of certain blessings and in the felt absence of His Presence, will we relax our determined grasp of our empty selves enough to appreciate His purposes...Through the pain of shattered dreams, God is

103

awakening us to the possibility of infinite pleasure. This is the nature of our journey; it's what the Spirit is doing. When we understand that, we'll define 'doing well' on this journey very differently than before.

Later in his book he writes this prayer:

Dear God, fill me with hope. I know You never promised me a rose garden, but I want to sense Your Presence with me as I walk through the weeds. Send Your Spirit to fill me with that unspeakable joy the Bible talks about. Grow the fruit of the Spirit in my soul. Please. I can't go on unless you do!

I really echo that prayer in my life, I need more of God and, as I pass significant birthdays as well as those in between, I want to see my life getting better in terms of my relationship with God. My physical circumstances keep changing as do my roles and I do believe that I am ready for all my heavenly Father is calling me to, and that includes knowing His joy. I love the fact that I am forever changing, forever learning and I still feel as though I am in my early 20s inside, so the world continues to be an exciting place to be, full of hope, full of eternity.

But it's not always like this, sometimes joy eludes me and then in my emptiness, in my misery of absent blessings, in my pain, I find a God shaped hole which only He can fill. He may not be there to fill it immediately but my desire for God deepens and I come to realise that life is so much more than my circumstances. We need Him; we are totally dependent on Him. I don't believe that as a sufferer of mental health problems I should think of myself as a victim, nor that others should think of me that way – my life's journey has taken me closer to God and my desire for Him is increasing; that has got to be good. God has given me many blessings in my life and I am grateful. He knows just how far I can go. Like Paul I must learn to be content whatever the circumstances:

> *I know what it is to be in need, and I know what it is to have plenty. I have learned the secret of being content in any and every situation, whether well fed or hungry, whether living in plenty or in want. I can do all this through him who gives me strength.* Philippians 4:12–13 TNIV

When my illness has been active, I cannot be content – that's part of the illness, but Abba has also provided me with help.

God's Wise Provision

Part of God's help for me came in the form of Bob, who I have referred to earlier. His psychotherapy sessions were not like those I had had before. Seeing him was rather like going for a confessional – I poured out with honesty my thoughts and feelings, knowing that with him I was not going to be judged. He was away from my home situation; it was intensely private and nothing said in the four walls of the room would go out of there except to Prof or to his own supervisor. (This is not the same situation for therapists or counsellors who are more usually independent and therefore the confidentiality rule would be absolute, but Bob is part of the Advanced Interventions Service, so he is part of 'the team'. More can be found about the talking therapies in the chapter 'Treatments and Therapies'.)

Bob does not know any of the people I want to talk about, except Phil of course, and, rather than being told how I have fallen from the beaten track, I am met with acceptance and understanding, even sympathy for my ways. So, unwittingly, this mirrors my heavenly Father, but whereas with Bob and the psychological methods he uses, I could be rightly called upon to let go of a negative mindset or have my wrong thinking challenged, it is the Spirit who highlights my sin and I am able to confess and repent, knowing I am not only accepted and understood, but forgiven. Bob has supported me through so much, as once out of hospital, various traumas and problems continued to arise and he would often show me how my reaction to them was not altogether healthy emotionally and I was able to translate the benefit of this into my spiritual life as well. For instance, when I was being retired from my job, I had to see an independent doctor to assess my fitness. I was scared; worried that he might think I was a fraud, (a very depressive reaction). Bob showed me that there was no need to be fearful, that I had nothing to hide and that the reports that had been written about me were all truthful. I in turn had to learn that it is not God's will for me to be afraid. 'The Lord is for me; I will not fear; what can man do to me?' (Psalm 118:6 NASB) Bob rehearsed with me the sort of questions I would be asked and God spoke to me and said 'Be strong and very courageous.' (Joshua 1:7)

About us as a Couple

When Phil and I first married I always thought I was the strong one, but a few years later a shock came my way. We were at a church meeting and there was a visiting couple talking on marriage. One of them had a word of knowledge and said 'there is a woman here who is not submitted to her husband and is saying in her heart that she could do better than him'. I was stunned, because those very thoughts had been in my mind earlier that day, so I trembled with fear as I accepted the invitation to make myself known and go up for prayer. The couple spoke kindly to both Phil and I. They shared with me how my feelings of superiority would destroy our marriage and that I needed to put it right with God. They explained that being submitted did not mean that the man has the right to 'Lord it over you' or to suppress you in any way, rather it would free him to become the head of the household, which in fact I so much desired, and it would bring us closer together. Since that time, Phil and I have learned to talk more openly and honestly with each other, to make shared decisions about important aspects of our lives, but I have always had the security that Phil has the final say if something important comes up and we are at loggerheads with one another. Needless to say that has never arisen as we have always managed to sort things out and hopefully always will, with the help of God. But when I have become ill, Phil naturally adopts the role of care giver and also is the one to make the decisions while I am 'away'. In my younger days, I would never have imagined that I was going to be the one afflicted with mental illness, let alone with such severity.

So, as I have grown spiritually, I have been at pains to share my experiences with Phil. During my sessions with Bob, when something comes up that I realise I have not discussed with Phil, I make sure I do so at some point, though not necessarily immediately. I do not do this out of compulsion, far from it, but I find that we have the sort of relationship where we don't need to keep secrets; it has been part of the healing to talk through issues which have been raised and I have been able to bring Bob's wisdom and insight to light as we wrestle with them further. We can then pray together as we seek the Father's healing for the wounds of the past. One of these issues has been that of self harm.

Aspects of Self Harm

In Southampton my self harm by cutting was very severe and on more than one occasion threatened my life. I remember little of my walk with God then except for the fact that I have a small Bible which remains marked on all sides with WIELD in thick black pen. I read the psalms one at a time through my time in the psychiatric intensive care unit, but my thinking was very slowed and my memory so poor that my recollection of those days is limited and I didn't leave any clues in my diary. When I had the relapse and was in hospital at the Carseview Centre in Dundee, I did not cut myself. I had needed plastic surgery to my abdomen after my recovery from the first Depression and I did not want to do that again. My self harm during this time had no consequences for other people, which at least did not bring me to the attention of A&E.

But I do remember how I left painful bruises on my body after a session of self flagellation. I still felt this was what I deserved; I could not equate my spiritual knowledge with the depths of my feelings. I felt I was the exception to the rule. I was saved yes, but I was still the sinner in filthy rags, I was still worthy of nothing except punishment. I compared myself to those in the third world who had nothing and that made me feel all the more disgusted with myself. I was so aware of how selfish and self centred I was, so everything about me seemed a total failure. I don't know if I thought God approved, I think I just didn't have anything but a simple faith that somehow He was with me even in the hospital; I was so full of guilt and despair, this act of aggression did little to affect my conscience.

There are all sorts of leaflets produced about self harm nowadays – as if this can all be understood by reading a leaflet. Back at the DOP in Southampton there is now a policy of 'dialectical behaviour therapy' for those who self harm –

basically the patients get optimal access to staff while they are not self harming, but when they do an act of self harm, it all stops. How long before you are classified as not self harming I wonder! So, once again, the usual situation within institutions exists – one size fits all. It wouldn't have fitted me.

No one talked to me after I self harmed; no one asked me how I felt or why I did it. It was as though if it were talked about I would do it again. But I did do it again, so why didn't they break the silence and ask me anyway? Even at Carseview that happened. One thing I do remember is the question, 'why don't you talk to us before you self harm?'. Well the truth is when I approached staff to say how bad I was feeling, more often than not I was told to distract myself – play some music, watch TV or I would be offered some lorazepam (a tranquiliser). They didn't get it – those things were only temporary stop gaps. Sometimes I would get a really switched on nurse; I remember one particular occasion when she ran a bubble bath for me, stayed with me to talk to me or another when I was given a hot drink, and she talked first and then popped back to see me later, to see how I was doing. I think that only happened once but I'm grateful for Dot – she cared!

Worse still was when I was handed an elastic band and told to flick it against my wrist to induce pain I tried it, I tried anything. It didn't work – there's no way that it relieved the deeply intense desire to hurt myself. People have all sorts of theories, they think they know it all and can glibly tell you that the reason you hurt yourself is to dull the pain of your brain. I know it, I know it full well. During the first episode of my depression, sometimes I used to sneak downstairs in the middle of the night; I remember now with horror that I used to boil the kettle and, I hardly dare say it, pour it on my arm. The pain was excruciating, how appalling – the subsequent burn certainly distracted me from the awful torment of my depression, but if the people who write the theories think that's the only reason they are sorely mistaken. I also had comfort in my pain, once the initial act was done, as I remembered Jesus. He knew what it was like for me: 'For we do not have a high priest who is unable to sympathise with our weaknesses, but we have one who has been tempted in every way, just as we are – yet was without sin.' (Hebrews 4:15)

I can only speak for myself and for years I have kept it buried. When I recovered from my first bout of depression, I could only look at my scars and wonder why on earth I did these things to myself. It seemed incomprehensible – it was incomprehensible – it still is incomprehensible, but now I have allowed myself to explore it from a safe distance where I am not going to get dragged in. I was always on the defensive when I heard that it was an attention seeking ploy, because that was so superficial, so judgemental, but as I think about it more, there is a small element of truth in that brash statement. But no, what I craved was not a trip to A&E or the attention poured out over the resulting wounds, but rather some analgesia for the intense pain, the unbearable pain that I was suffering right in the centre of my being. It was almost a statement. '*You* can't do this to yourself, torture yourself physically, but it is easy for me, because that pain is nothing, no nothing compared to what is going on in my head. Help me, please help me.' But help never came. It is true that the physical act of self harm brought some temporary relief until the unbearable tension rose again, but it also brought a resignation to my isolation. My isolation was reinforced by others dealing only with the physical wound without giving any attention to the deep source of extravagant suffering where no other human being was able to accompany me. But my heavenly Father was there with me, I know that now, I was not alone.

The same was true for the suicide attempts – after I was dealt with medically, or even during the time I was having treatment, no one asked the question 'why'? They all thought they knew the reason already; after all I was an inpatient receiving treatment for major depression – no need to find out any more. I remember lying in the A&E ward with a drip in my arm as I received treatment, the vomiting at last abated, with and there was no thought whatsoever given to my mental state. I was too exhausted to rebel and remove the drip. All I wanted was to get back to the psychiatric ward, away from the world of white sheets and monitors and blood pressures and charts. No nurse actually talked to me except to ask how much I had drunk or to tell me to place the thermometer under my tongue. Meantime all the thoughts about why I had tried to end my life, why I had failed, what others would think of me, whether I would be punished when I got back to the ward, went round and round and round and round in my head. I was so tired but I could not sleep. Then at last I would be told I was out of danger, only by less dramatic words. 'Treatment is complete. You can return to the ward.' I had no shoes, no clothes, no hair brush, nothing to dignify myself with. The ward was called and a nursing assistant is sent to fetch me armed with a pair of shoes. 'Oh' she would say, 'I didn't know you had no clothes, well never mind, a dressing gown will have to do!' My humility was completed as I walked through the waiting room free to go and get locked back into the psychiatric ward. I felt the eyes of curiosity of the anxious waiting room like hot pokers boring into my face and head as I was escorted out without sympathy by the sane woman distinguished by her uniform.

Once back at the unit, the escort was not complete until I was taken to my room and informed that from now on I would be 'on obs' (being under the direct observation of a nurse, 24 hours a day.) Still no one asked how I was, that hot drink was still elusive and once again I returned to the silence, to the isolation of those, by now, accusing and regretful thoughts. I longed for a meal time when at least one of the other patients may break the silence by asking what had happened and I could satisfy my friend by describing the events of those last 24 hours in clinical detail, of course not revealing anything of the dreadful loneliness and exquisite pain deep in my soul. The distraction came again, this time in the fight to get set free from the obs. It was a delicate balance, on the one hand I was looking forward to the visit from my doctor – maybe I would at last have the opportunity to share the depths of my suffering – but on the other hand the desire to be free from the imposition of the chattering nurses was also high on the agenda. But once again, 'the episode' was not asked about, so I just buried it deeper into the file in my psyche which is padlocked with a notice, 'unlock at your peril'.

The punitive nature of these assaults on my life was revealed to me during the privacy of an interaction with my therapist, Bob. He showed me that, once again, it is brought to the forefront of my mind because, while I act out, I am not conscious that that is precisely what I am doing. My blatant disregard for my self-preservation instinct is exposed by the ferocity of the acts of barbarism I carry out against my poor defenceless body. I don't hate it, the physical form, but rather myself, my mind, body and soul. I no longer remember that I am fearfully and wonderfully made, that I was made in secret and skilfully wrought in the depths of the earth. I have become the personification of evil, I deserve all I am going to get, but then somehow the child in me responds, the lost, lonely, fearful child and she wants her mummy and her daddy and she doesn't know where to find them. The attack ceases and the want of comfort remains until once again I find myself in the terrifying clutches of ordinary life, filled with real people who are ready to apportion blame, to mistrust my motives, to label me as one of those – 'self harmers'.

God is Still With Me

I know there is a question every Christian is longing to ask – 'where was God in all of this?'. As I say, when I was severely depressed, I still had an awareness that God was there and, during the rare attempts I have made on my life, I was still convinced that I was going home to be with Jesus and the Father. I never did this lightly, or for anything less than death, but it always 'went wrong'. Fortunately my chaotic and befuddled brain didn't manage to give me the clarity and reason to carry out a fatal attack. Was that not in God's hands? I know Christians who have taken their lives and that is very much a tragedy, as every suicide is, but fortunately for me, I have been blessed with continued life, even though the saving gave me no reason to believe that was the case at the time.

When I was discharged, I continued to self harm at intervals when my mood lowered again, but I was also able to say to myself the words of Habakkuk 3:17–19 (NASB):

Though the fig tree should not blossom
And there be no fruit on the vines
Though the yield of the olive should fail
And the fields produce no food,
Though the flock should be cut off from the fold
And there be no cattle in the stalls,
Yet I will exult in the Lord
I will rejoice in the God of my salvation.
God, the Lord be my strength.

I started to praise God again, and this was the beginning of my spiritual recovery as well as my emotional recovery, but, like the depression, it was not without its setbacks. I still had a low self esteem and, though Bob tried to bolster it with the encouragements of what I had managed to achieve despite the unquestionable difficulties I have had to face, I went back time and time again to the fact that these were only possible because of God. I took the view that my self esteem relies on the fact that I am loved so much that Jesus was sent to die for me, but I myself am of no value in myself apart from that.

While part of this is true, it is not the whole truth. We are all 'fearfully and wonderfully made' (Psalm 139:14), whether we acknowledge this or not. In our human-ness, even in our sinful nature, we are of value – otherwise why would Jesus have died for us? We were 'bought at a price' (1 Corinthians 6:20), God is not 'wanting anyone to perish, but everyone to come to repentance' (2 Peter 3:9). We have intrinsic value for who we are, not what we can do, but this head knowledge had not gone down to my heart. Furthermore we are adopted into God's family, God is more than just 'the' Father, He is **our Father**, He is **my Father**.

There are still some within the church who don't know this, I didn't know this until I was taught the truth; they continue trying to please God, their bosses, their friends, their parents in the hope that this might give them value. But God's grace is such – He gives to us, but we don't deserve anything. We don't need to earn His love and acceptance; our works will never be good enough. He gives it to us anyway and though Bob is doing his job as a professional, God was showing me through Him, that I did not need to impress Him one little bit yet I was accepted. Bizarre though it may seem, I needed the same revelation of God's love and grace just as the person who works in order to earn it does. Slowly, as I continued my recovery, at last the time came where I was able to say 'I don't need to hurt myself anymore, I no longer need punishment, Jesus paid the price to set me free. He loves me, yes even me!' Then as I encountered Mark Stibbe's message about God being our Father and that we are adopted into His family, and now I can truly say 'I am the Father's child, He loves me, yes even me!'. Our triune God is not complete without mention of the Holy Spirit, He wants to dwell in me, yes even me!

9: A Brief History of Mental Illness

This will not be a comprehensive account of the history of mental illness or the history of psychiatry. Instead I have chosen to write about some of the history just to illustrate to you firstly the different ways people have been treated, but also why there is such an understandable fear of becoming one of the mentally ill, which has been handed down from generation to generation.

'Mental illness', the term we use today, has always been with us as a human race just as ageing, decay, disease and death have been present from the time of the fall. It is difficult to know what the earliest historical evidence for this is. The trephining of the skull, which is evident in the fossilised remains of Stone Age man, has been linked as a treatment for insanity; however I cannot defend this point of view since I am not a historian. But there are many writings preserved from the ancient Greeks and other cultures describing states which sound remarkably similar to modern descriptions of different mental illnesses. In these documents descriptions of the causes, often linked to deities or demons, are included as are the treatments, which were variously humane and kind or punitive and barbaric.

It was Hippocrates, born in 460BC, who seemed to be the first person to write that he believed that disease states had natural causes as opposed to the more common belief at the time that they were afflictions sent by the gods. His theories of disease, which included insanity and madness, was that undigested residues were produced by unsuitable diet and that these residues excreted vapours, which passed into the

116

body generally and produced diseases; his view was highly influential in the treatment of disorders during that time. Insanity and madness have been the terms used to describe mental conditions, but Hippocrates also described other states such as melancholia, which he said was caused by 'black bile'. He has long been known as the 'Father of Medicine' and it is from him that the Hippocratic Oath arises.

Following Hippocrates there were various famous 'physicians' or philosophers arising in the Greek and Roman worlds. The Greek physician Asclepiades advocated that disorders we now consider to be mental illnesses were treated with fresh air, light, appropriate diet, bathing, massage and exercise in order to restore harmony. On the other hand a Roman called Cornelius Celsus who lived around the time of Christ (25BC–50AD) advocated the use of anything that 'thoroughly agitates the spirit' and used starvation, restraint in chains and whipping to treat the same conditions.

Bible Times

In Jesus' day, it is easy to conclude that mental disturbance or illness was widespread as described by these early documents, but since there were no 'medical treatments' some of the extremes of these illnesses would have been seen and presumably some of these would have been labelled as insanity and madness. Both insanity and madness are referred to in both the Old and New Testaments, but it is notable that Jesus did not single this out for special mention when He healed people or when He cast out demons. From this I conclude, not surprisingly, that Jesus had no problem with what we now call mental illness. We also know that Jesus 'healed many of those who were ill with various diseases' (Mark 1:34) and 'At that very time Jesus cured many who had

117

diseases, sicknesses and evil spirits' (Luke 7:21). So it's fair to say that the mentally ill would have been among the ones healed, even more so because at that time the artificial distinction between 'mental' and 'physical' disease had not been made.

In fact there are only two mentions of the word 'insane' that occur in the New Testament. One was when Jesus Himself was described by His opponents as being insane, 'many of them were saying (of Jesus) "he has a demon and is insane."' (John 10:20 NASB) The other is when Paul describes himself in 2 Corinthians 11:23 'are they servants of Christ? (I am out of my mind talking like this). I am more...' When Paul makes his defence to Agrippa, Festus, who is also present, says 'Paul, you are out of your mind! Your great learning is driving you insane.' (Acts 26:24), indicating that there was clear recognition of 'mental illness' within society at that time.

Later there was a famous physician, Soranus of Ephesus (2nd century AD), who was a pioneer in the treatment of mental disorders. He has been described as giving sufferers light, airy conditions and said that they were not to be beaten. He recommended that those suffering from nervous ailments should drink the alkaline waters of the town. We now know that those waters contained high levels of the ion Lithium, which was rediscovered in 1949 by an Australian psychiatrist called John Cade as a treatment for mania and depressive disorders.

Abusive Attitudes in Britain

The more enlightened treatments for sufferers of mental disorders varied down the ages and by the Middle Ages in Europe more primitive thinking about mental illness once again came to the forefront. Then witchcraft and demon possession were thought to be the causes of madness or insanity and with this came barbaric treatments. If sufferers were thought to be demon possessed they were often tortured mercilessly to make the body unfit for the demon. It was felt that the salvation of the soul was far more important than allowing a demon to dwell within the body.

It seems that the mentally ill were largely cared for by their families as long as they were not considered to be violent or dangerous. From the 16th–18th centuries some of the mentally disturbed may have been the victims of witch hunts, but the idea of confinement of the insane became established in society. Within Britain, the insane were often admitted to workhouses, poorhouses or jailed. As early as 1337 the first ever psychiatric hospital, the Bethlem Royal Hospital, opened its gates to the mentally ill. At first the conditions were good and there was a badge that inmates at the hospital wore on their clothes, which meant they could be returned to the hospital if they went out. But some time later conditions were appalling and inmates were chained to the floor or to the walls. Various contraptions were used including the spinning stool, to 'rearrange the contents of the brain', and restraints in the form of elaborate strait jackets, which kept patients either fixed to the wall or fixed to a chair. Whipping and beatings were also meted out to the insane not just at this time but in many of the eras in which madness was felt to be due to moral failure, or for the sins of being possessed or for being a witch. The Bethlem hospital changed over time and at one point it is thought that those who were not violent or felt to be a danger were given a licence to beg. In the latter part of the 18th century, the public could pay a penny to go and watch inmates as a form of entertainment.

Around the same time, private madhouses came into being in Britain. They were privately owned establishments which were run as businesses for the reception and treatment of the insane. Most were relatively small and cared for up to 25 patients. William Battie was the founder of St Luke's hospital in London in 1751 and he also owned two private madhouses. He wrote the 'Treatise on Madness' in which he said:

Madness is...as manageable as many other distempers, which are equally dreadful and obstinate, and yet are not looked upon as incurable; such unhappy objects ought by no means to be abandoned, much less shut up in loathsome prisons as criminals or nuisances to the society.

It is hard to know what kind of conditions inmates were kept in the private madhouses; it is known that 'paupers' were admitted and paid for by their parishes. The fact that there were some with appalling conditions is known as in 1774 an Act for Regulating Madhouses was passed after a public outcry concerning one or two establishments. In the worst conditions, paupers were crowded in ill-ventilated cells in converted outbuildings, half naked on filthy straw. But it is believed that these extreme conditions were not the norm, as many flourished as businesses and people were expected to be cured after a stay in them. Even the Bethlem hospital would not keep its inmates for more than a year.

We know that when the asylums came to be established, the wealthy were often housed in stately homes with extensive grounds and given recreation and had music rooms, good diet and exercise. As usual it was the poor who had to suffer the worst conditions.

At the end of the 18th century, two physicians came to the fore – William Tuke, a Quaker, and a French man by the name of Phillipe Pinel. They brought a more enlightened and humane 'psychosocial' approach to the care of the insane. It wasn't until the 19th century, though, that sufferers became known as patients and the concept of 'mental illness' was born.

The Age of Asylums

It was also in the early 19th century that the massive development of the asylums happened in Britain. They were supposed to be the answer to the scandalous overcrowding and conditions occurring in the private 'madhouses' and they were designed to provide recreational spaces with 'free circulation of air' for several hundred inmates. Although insanity and other nervous complaints had become known as treatable conditions, it was recognised that a category, the 'incurable lunatic', existed. Unfortunately, the asylums were soon to become overcrowded and understaffed. The able were conscripted into a labour force to run the asylum but those who were too ill suffered neglect and inactivity, increasing the effects of the inertia and apathy produced by the illness itself. Families were ashamed of having a 'lunatic' as one of their members and many of them would commit a mentally ill relative to the care of the asylum. It was not expected that those who were seriously disturbed would come out. It was not until the 1940s that there was any major attempt to discharge patients back to the community. But then in the 1950s various medications were produced which hastened discharge, especially for those who had psychotic illnesses like schizophrenia that, until then, had remained untreatable. However these patients became conspicuous in the community because of the awful side effects of the new drugs – they shuffled in their walking, had shaking arms and hands, spasms of the head, neck and tongue and difficulty in speech. The excessive saliva produced led to dribbling and so a new image of 'the mad' was formed.

Interestingly the stigma of the mentally ill was expressed more often by women than men, and more so by women with children as they felt the need to 'protect' their offspring. The rejection of these sufferers by society led directly to social isolation and therefore the self segregation of those with mental health problems. Lack of work led to poverty and so this vulnerable group of people became more noticeable by their shabby and un-fashionable clothing and the movement disorders as already mentioned. Sheltered housing is often needed for ex-patients who are only partially independent and these could be opposed by angry citizens who thought of them as dangerous and unpredictable. The local papers would side with those who had the modern distinction of NIMBYs – not in my back yard. The cycle of stigma continues.

It is worth knowing that during the rule of the Nazis in Germany and other European nations, an estimated 200,000 mentally ill patients were exterminated along with the Jews (and some active Christians). Also inmates of mental hospitals have at times been subject to forced sterilisation. Although this did not happen in Britain, there was a widespread belief that incarceration within an asylum would at least take these unfortunates out of society and therefore prevent them from 'breeding' – thereby preventing the propagation of hereditary causes of insanity.

The Law and Mental Illness

It was only relatively recently that suicide was decriminalised in the UK, with the suicide act of 1961. The notion of care in the community was first muted in this same year also and there followed the emptying of the great psychiatric institutions where patients had been interned for life – sadly in some cases with little or no provision for ongoing care and with little or no preparation for life in the outside world. The 1990 NHS and Community Care Act was intended to decrease unnecessary institutionalisation, and further discharges of long term patients occurred. Now it is only the acutely unwell or those waiting for placement in special accommodation that are found in psychiatric hospitals. There are no long stay wards left.

It was also relatively recently that drugs were made available to treat the major disorders (1950/60s) such as depression and schizophrenia. They have been constantly refined since then and much progress has been made, even in the last two decades, to find drugs which are more tolerable than the old ones, but even the newer drugs are not free from side effects.

It is therefore not surprising that mental illness has been greatly feared over the years, as it is clearly associated with psychiatric institutions, barbaric treatments and also with the belief that once you have a mental illness you never get better. So fear is endemic in our national (UK wide) cultures.

Stigma can also provide society with a scape goat; 'those' people – ones with mental illness – are the abnormal ones and therefore everyone else can be confident that they are the normal ones. If you think about it, this is also true for other prejudices, such as racism, sexism and homophobia.

The above prejudices are being tackled by society and name calling is definitely considered wrong, but, despite campaigns to educate the public about mental health issues, no such 'political correctness' exists. Some terms are outdated, but are quickly replaced by others, such as looney, nutter, headcase, weirdo, someone may be bonkers, crazy, batty, a head case, mental or described as 'he's lost his marbles'. We use these terms in common parlance often in a very light hearted way and I am not suggesting that we should not do so at all, but it is highly offensive to refer to a mentally ill person, or persons, by such derogatory terms.

I hope this brief history has been helpful in just understanding that the segregation of the mentally ill, particularly those deemed insane has happened for a very long time in our culture. It is no wonder that stigma is so entrenched in our society. But this is not just an inherent ill, there is a spiritual side to it as well. God our Father loves those who are poor and weak, just as much as those who are rich and strong, maybe more so, and the devil would have us believe that not everyone is valuable in God's eyes. As we understand more of the Father's love for ourselves and for others whatever their condition, we will be able to embrace anyone who crosses our path rich or poor, weak or strong, sick or well, in good mental health or in poor mental health.

10: Demon Possession – is there any Link with Mental Illness?

If you don't believe in the spiritual life, then the notion of demon possession is absurd and ludicrous. But as Christians we believe that we are made up of body, mind and soul or spirit (Matthew 22:37). We believe in God. Satan was a fallen angel, a leader of some importance in the angelic host who rebelled against God and departed from Him taking other fallen angels with him, which are now known as demons or evil spirits.

Of course none of this can be proven scientifically; but we believe the Bible and as Paul says in his letter to the Corinthians, talking of Christ's resurrection, 'If only for this life we have hope in Christ, we are to be pitied more than all men.' (1 Corinthians 15:19) In other words if Jesus was put to death just as any individual and did not in fact rise again, we are truly deceived. But we do believe! The Bible is full of proofs and we live by faith, which is part of our living experience of Jesus today.

It is evident throughout the Gospels that there were people who were under the influence of demons or who had a demon. Translated from the Greek, (the language that the New Testament was written in), we see this referred to as being 'possessed' by a demon. Jesus was the first person in His day to have authority over demons (Mark 1:27) and is described in all the Gospels not only as healing the sick but also setting people free by casting out demons.

We also know that Satan, though he is described variously as 'the devil', 'the evil one', 'the serpent', 'Beelzebub' or 'the prince of this world', stands condemned (John 16:11). Jesus has absolute authority over Satan and all his demons; He passed this authority and power to His twelve disciples to heal the sick and to drive out demons. Then later Jesus appointed the 72 and sent them out likewise. When they returned from their ministry trip into the world, they returned with joy saying 'Lord, even the demons submit to us in your name' and Jesus replied, 'I saw Satan fall like lightning from heaven'. (Luke 10:18) But ultimately the victory was gained at the cross when Jesus broke the power of the devil. (Hebrews 2:14)

Demon possession was also described in the Bible after Jesus' death and resurrection, when Paul was followed by a slave girl who had a spirit by which she predicted the future, shouting 'these men are servant of the Most High God who are telling you the way to be saved'. This carried on for many days and finally Paul got so annoyed that he cast the spirit out (Acts 16:18).

Philip is also described in Acts as performing signs with his preaching, which included freeing people from demons (Acts 8:7).

So how was demon possession described and what makes Christians today believe that those with mental illness could be possessed? I was never accused of being demon possessed while I was ill, for which I am very grateful – I can only imagine that in my depressed state I would have taken it very badly. Again I would have thought that it was my fault and that I must have opened myself in some way to allow the demon in. It would definitely have made me more liable to blame myself. However, when I recovered, I was asked the question of whether I thought the mentally ill were demon possessed. The friend who asked me was genuine. She was leaning towards the attitude that yes, that is the case, and she did not have any explanation for my illness. As always we need to learn from history and the fact that when sicknesses involving the mind were blamed on demon possession the sufferers were tortured and sometimes killed, whereas when the sickness was seen to be 'suffering', then patients were treated kindly and with mercy and nursed back to recovery.

We know, as I have said before, that the Scriptures are just as relevant today as they were to the first Christians and we have the added advantage of having the New Testament written down for us today. There is no reason to assume that this was just relevant to those first century Christians, if that were the case, the Bible would say so! Matthew 4:24 says this:

News about Him (Jesus) spread all over Syria and people brought to Him all who were ill with various diseases, those suffering severe pain, the demon-possessed, those having seizures and the paralysed; and he healed them.

Then there are more specific examples, like that of a woman who had been crippled by a spirit (demon) for 18 years. She was bent over and could not straighten up at all. Jesus said to her, 'Woman, you are set free from your infirmity'. Then He put His hands on her and immediately she straightened up and praised God. (Luke 13:13) There was not a lot of fuss or bother; Jesus just got the job done! Another example is the famous one which is often quoted to say that those with epilepsy are demon possessed – Matthew 17:14:

...a man approached Jesus and knelt before Him. 'Lord, have mercy on my son', he said. 'He has seizures and is suffering greatly. He often falls into the fire or into the water. I brought him to your disciples, but they could not heal him.' 'You unbelieving and perverse generation,' Jesus replied, 'How long will I stay with you? How long will I put up with you? Bring the boy to me.' Jesus rebuked the demon, and it came out of the boy, and he was healed from that moment.

Yet as I have quoted from Matthew, there were others who had seizures who were simply just healed. It's important to note as well, that Jesus rebuked the demon, not the boy. In the version of the same story in Mark 9, the boy is also described as mute and when Jesus rebukes the demon he addresses it as 'You deaf and mute spirit', which He commands to come out of the boy and never enter him again. Why is it then that the same people who say epileptics are demon possessed do not suggest that the deaf are also? Now I am not saying they should, but this is a scriptural example of an evil spirit causing those symptoms too.

The Gadarene Demoniac

Then there is the example of the man from the region of the Gadarenes, known as the 'Gadarene demoniac' often used as the basis for which people claim that those with mental illness are possessed. This is Luke's Gospel version of the event (Luke 8:27–29):

> When Jesus stepped ashore, he was met by a demon-possessed man from the town. For a long time this man had not worn clothes or lived in a house, but had lived in the tombs. When he saw Jesus, he cried out and fell at his feet, shouting at the top of his voice, 'What do you want with me, Jesus, Son of the Most High God? I beg you, don't torture me!' For Jesus had commanded the evil spirit to come out of the man. Many times it had seized him and though he was chained hand and foot and kept under guard, he had broken his chains and had been driven by the demon into solitary places.

In Mark's version he is also described as gashing himself with stones and in Matthew's version, which describes two men, they are so violent that no one could pass that way. Does this describe mental illness? It does describe 'self harm', but it certainly doesn't describe a particular diagnosis and mental illness is not nebulous; it consists of distinct and separate groups of symptoms and signs. Nor does it describe anyone in my experience that I have known either as a patient or as a doctor, who has been referred to mental health services. However when the demons, known as 'Legion' come out of the man the townspeople find him seated next to Jesus 'dressed and in his right mind' (Luke 8:35).

He had obviously been in terrible torment or distress from the accounts given of him; you might find him in a high security prison today for his violence or, if he was lucky, being assessed in a high security forensic unit in care of mental health services. But as I said before they would be struggling to come up with a diagnosis. Basically all that can be said is this describes a man who was possessed by many demons, not someone who was mentally ill. Long term tranquilisers were not going to cure his problem!

The Purpose of Scripture

I wonder why this passage is described in the Bible and why the story of the demon-possessed boy is described? Knowing that the Bible is just as relevant today as it has been for all time, I think that it is unlikely that the Holy Spirit was directing these stories to be written just for western, 21st century diagnoses to be made. He had other things in mind. The demon-possessed boy's story goes on to talk about his father's and the disciples' faith. In fact what the father said to Jesus when challenged was 'I do believe; help me overcome my unbelief!' This is one of my favourite verses, which I often echo in my prayer life – particularly when tempted to doubt.

As for the Gadarene Demoniac, the story tells of the Legion of demons entering the swine feeding on the hillside that then rush down the steep bank into the lake and are drowned. It tells of the local people's reaction of fear and rejection towards Jesus and how the healed man himself wants to follow Jesus. So there are many reasons why these accounts have been included in Scripture.

What I am saying is that there is no reason to conclude therefore that all mental illness or indeed epilepsy is caused by demon possession and to have a blanket attitude of this premise is wrong. What I am *not* saying is that mental illness or the symptoms of mental illness can *never* be caused by demonic influence. There may be times when it is entirely appropriate to rebuke the said demon in the name of Jesus or command it to leave, (although this should be left to someone with experience in this area). However this is *no more* likely than for any other sickness, illness or disability. Furthermore a Christian cannot be possessed by a demon as he or she is filled with God's Spirit when they are saved, however I do believe that they can be **oppressed** by one. Don't we often say 'they have asked Jesus into their life'? That they can be under the influence or attack of a demon or even the devil is without doubt and this can affect any one of us, particularly where we allow ourselves to sin. Even Jesus who was without sin was tempted in the wilderness for 40 days by Satan. Paul, who agonised over his 'thorn in the flesh', which he describes as a messenger of Satan, was tormented but he knew it was sent to him in order for him not to become conceited.

We are urged to 'Submit yourselves, then, to God. Resist the devil, and he will flee from you' (James 4:7). To 'be alert and of sober mind as the devil prowls round like a roaring lion looking for someone to devour' (1 Peter 5:8 TNIV) and to 'put on the whole armour of God, so that you can stand against the devil's schemes' (Ephesians 6:11). Verse 12 goes on to say 'For our struggle is not against flesh and blood, but against the rulers, against the authorities, against the powers of this dark world and against the spiritual forces of evil in the heavenly realms.'

In other words, Satan and demons are real and we are often called to do battle with them, rather than with people. However Jesus Christ is the victor and so we do not have any reason to fear them. Any notion that the sick person who comes to your church or that you happen to meet in the course of your life is first and foremost demon possessed needs to be quashed, particularly is the person is suffering from mental illness. If, however, you still suspect it after time or a spiritually mature person, especially one who has the gift of discerning of spirits, confirms it then deliverance may be required. This is to be a thing of gentleness with great care and respect given to the person in question. There is no need for this to be made public, no need for shouting, no need for blame and this is not the time for the inexperienced Christian to be 'trying out' their skills at spiritual warfare. We need to think of ourselves and how we are when we are ill, to think about how we would like to be treated. We are all called to pray for the sick (see James 5:13–16) and in verse 16 James says: 'Therefore confess your sins to each other and pray for each other so that you may be healed. The prayer of a righteous person is powerful and effective.' So we do well not to neglect the power of prayer. It is interesting to note that Jesus wasn't always there in person when someone was set free from demon possession. The Canaanite woman who asks Jesus to heal her daughter who is 'demon possessed and suffering terribly' argues her case: 'Then Jesus said to her, "Woman, you have great faith! Your request is granted." And her daughter was healed from that very hour.' Matthew 15:28 (TNIV)

An Inspired Article

I would like to quote Jonathan Clark, Manager of Premier Lifeline and a Director of Mind and Soul, in his talk 'Demons: Do they? Don't they? What if?':

So what about today? How does this apply in the twenty-first century and our science-based mental health services? I have worked in Mental Health for 27 years and have been involved in detaining people against their will for assessment and treatment. I have not had qualms about recommending people take their psychiatric medication and undergo therapy. If a person has a clearly diagnosed mental disorder that needs treating then I am convinced we should all support this treatment, whether professionals, community or Church. Yet I do not want to exclude the power of prayer. I have seen the impact of prayer ministry and Christian healing in the way God has transformed lives. Nor do I deny that demons still exist and in some cases there may be a need for the deliverance ministry. My greatest concern is that we all need wisdom to know when to treat, when to pray and when to deliver. We also need to ensure that all is done with respect to the individual, by experienced and competent practitioners under supervision and, where appropriate, in consultation with the other professional and support networks involved.

11: Hearing Voices

I have heard from a number of Christians that they feel a real dilemma when they are asked by their GP or psychiatrist whether or not they hear voices. After all Christians should be able to hear from God and many do so in a very personal way, so they could rightly say 'yes, I hear the voice of God'. Now what does that mean? And what do psychiatrists mean? Can the two ever be confused?

I would say I hear God speaking to me and I have also heard voices when I was ill. I am readily able to distinguish between the two, but I will try and explain my experiences to you in more detail.

When I hear God speaking to me it occurs in a number of ways. I have not, so far, heard God speak audibly but have read accounts of people and know of those who have. Hearing an audible voice was not unusual in the Bible; think of Samuel the boy who was living in the temple under the care and training of Eli the priest. God calls him by name while he is in bed, and three times he gets up and goes to Eli saying 'here I am, you called me'. It takes a while for Eli to realise that it is the Lord who is calling him, but finally Eli is able to tell Samuel to say to God, 'Speak, for your servant is listening'. Then God goes on to reveal his plan for Eli's household to Samuel. (1 Samuel 3:4–14)

Then in the New Testament, another example of someone hearing an audible voice is Saul, (Paul's name before he is converted), as he travels along the road to Damascus in pursuit of the Christians. He not only sees the risen Christ but hears him saying 'Saul, Saul why do you persecute me?'. Jesus identifies Himself and goes on to give Saul instructions. Saul's travelling companions are rendered speechless because they hear the voice but do not see anybody. (Acts 9:4–7)

How I Hear God

I tend to hear God in my thoughts. How do I know it's God and 'not just me'? Well, I cannot take ownership of these sort of 'thoughts', they are quiet and peaceable and may cut across what I happen to be thinking about. They are consistent with Scripture and my understanding of God's nature. Sometimes I may hear a statement such as 'I love you Cathy' or sometimes a gentle rebuke. We even have whole conversations. These tend to be in normal everyday language, not in special religious language. Do I think I might get it wrong? Undoubtedly I do sometimes as I am a beginner at tuning in and listening to God's voice; but I have as much faith that God will speak as I have of God allowing me to make mistakes, stepping in to make sure I don't do anything disastrous. He gives wisdom to all who ask for it and therefore I would require confirmation that it is actually God speaking to me if anything I believe He is saying is directional. It may be God, the Father, Jesus or the Holy Spirit speaking and I am not sure I can rightly identify who it is all the time!

God also speaks through the Bible when I read it, maybe highlighting a verse or leading me to read a particular passage. Basically God speaks in innumerable ways, through music, through preaching, through reading, through art, through other people and through creation, to name some examples. These need not be 'Christian' materials or Christian people either; God can use any situation, anywhere and at any time. My prayer is that I will hear Him more, because I want to be like Jesus and only do what I see the Father doing (John

5:19). James' exhortation 'everyone should be quick to listen, slow to speak and slow to become angry' (James 1:19) is not just a recommendation for counsellors, but it is to all of us and part of that listening must surely be to God. This is not to say that professional counsellors only listen; far from it, many of them go through extensive training and use psychological techniques in diagnosis and as part of their therapy.

I'm not saying I am there yet, I certainly am not and I like to read and study books about listening to God. He is the great communicator; after all He created us and walked in the garden with Adam and Eve. It is the Fall that separated us from God and has made it so hard for us to hear Him in our usual, unsaved state. Watch a young child, they are so open to praying; it is so natural for them, they haven't learned any hindrances to this activity yet; belief in God and talking to God can be so easy for little ones. I did not have that benefit when I was small but, even at the age of 14 when I first heard the gospel, I did not feel the need to question it or analyse the psychology of it. My very real experience of the release from the guilt that was weighing me down was evidence enough for me to believe.

We are all on a spiritual journey and we have no reason to compete with each other or show off about where we are with God, because it is not by any merit of ourselves that we are where we are but rather by that amazing gift to us, the grace of God. However I think all of us should consider being open to hearing the voice of God. He is, after all, our Father who loved us so much that He sent Jesus to die for us, to **open the way for us to have a real relationship with Him** and we all know that the essence of a good relationship is good communication.

Back to the Clinic

So would I answer yes if I was asked whether I was hearing voices? For all of the experiences I have just told you about the answer would be 'no'. My spiritual life is not what the doctor wants to know about. S/he is not trained in spiritual things and, so whether or not s/he is Christian believer, from any other faith or an atheist is totally irrelevant. Having said that, a Christian doctor is much more likely to understand what you mean if you were to say you heard from God.

Now there are certain disorders within the diagnoses of mental illness that can take on the form of religious delusions or experiences.

One of my friends just happened to have a breakdown in my kitchen, when she brought her children over to play with mine. During this time she fell down on her knees on the kitchen floor, outstretched her arms and invoked the name of the Lord. She may have been having a profound spiritual experience, that I shall never know, but what I do know is that she was doing all this with totally no attention to her children. Her thoughts and ideas were not rational and the family's basic needs were not being met. She needed accompanying to the doctor rather than encouraging to seek God or hear His voice! Unfortunately she required a period in hospital and, in her usual state, this behaviour was most abnormal. She did however fully recover from this and went back to being her normal, lovely self.

More seriously, though, there are those who believe that they have a hotline to God or believe that they actually are God or Jesus, but these poor patients will have other abnormalities in their thought patterns as well which will be seen by the doctor. For instance they may believe that they can control the world or have outrageous supernatural powers.

I too was in a very bad way when I did hear voices. I was in the general hospital in Southampton after a failed suicide attempt when I started to hear voices telling me what a bad person I was. They were so real and their accusations seemed so accurate that I was greatly distressed and pulled back the curtain around my bed to tell them to stop, but there was no one there. I was desperate to tell my doctors about it, I was not in the least bit shy or embarrassed; it was an awful experience and was part of the psychotic depression that I was experiencing. The doctors needed to know about it as it was treatable and indeed was relieved when they made a change to my medication.

Not all patients are so forthcoming. People can be ashamed, particularly when what they hear is unpleasant, abusive or sexual in nature, but others can be quite open about what they are hearing. For some the experience is new, as it was for me, but for others who have been ill for a long time, they may find that hearing voices is part of their everyday experience. Voices usually occur in the context of a so-called psychotic illness and in fact, along with other symptoms, help to make the diagnosis clear. This is why doctors ask questions about hearing voices. But were you to answer 'yes' with regard to your experience of hearing God, it is unlikely to be mistaken for symptoms of psychotic illness in isolation without any other symptoms and signs supporting it. However, it may make your doctor view you with wariness or scepticism, or make the note that you are eccentric – just as any other member of the public would who knows nothing of the realities of a spiritual life in Christ.

So are you being honest to answer 'no' to the question of 'do you hear voices' if you are one of those Christians who does actually hear an audible voice from God? I am definitely of the opinion that you should be honest with your doctors. How can they possibly help you if you are keeping back information; you cannot always tell what is relevant for them to know about or not? However if you do want to tell them about hearing an audible voice of God, it would definitely be worth saying that this is normal within the Christian Church, describe the circumstances in which it occurs and, if the doctor would like to know more about it, it would be very helpful if you would be willing for him/her to chat to your minister/elder or a trusted friend.

Hearing Voices

What about the people who do hear voices? I understand that for some this is thought to be a manifestation of demon possession. I caution against this view, however, and refer back to the chapter on demon possession. Hearing voices is a symptom of many psychotic illnesses including schizophrenia, but also can be a feature of mania (the 'high' phase of bipolar disorder) and also, as with me, depression when severe. This can be extremely distressing and at the very least highly unpleasant and irritating. For those sufferers with chronic (longstanding) schizophrenia, it can become an ongoing symptom that never goes away and there may be a greater or lesser degree of acceptance then. Rarely, you may see the person conversing with the voices – once again this is not a sign of demon possession, although it is classically described as 'madness'. The person concerned is very ill and needs our care and compassion, not condemnation. Having said that, there are some amazing people with schizophrenia who manage their own illness so well, and have to live with the voices in order not to be overmedicated.

Imagine leaving the television or radio on loudly when you are trying to have an intimate conversation with just one other person in the room – you may be able to ignore it, but more than likely you would turn it off. Most parents will know how frustrating it is to have their child butt in when they are speaking on the phone or simply talking to someone else and they will often say 'not now, I'll talk to you later'. Well the person hearing voices does not have the luxury of being able to turn it off. They have a literal voice or voices as loud and as real as any person's voice, speaking at them or to them or about them, often all the time. The voice may comment on their actions, argue with their conversation or even order them about. The voices in depression tend to be derogatory voices, speaking directly at the sufferer saying such things like 'you deserve to be dead'. It is very difficult for the hearer of voices to take part in conversation, as they are often distracted or wary. For this symptom and others, a psychiatrist will prescribe drugs which should help lessen these experiences or even abolish them altogether.

If you would like to, try this practical exercise. You need three people; have two of them sit in chairs facing each other and begin a conversation whilst the third person whispers continually in one of the converser's ear. They can say anything, but to make it more realistic it would be good to try just questioning the conversation that's taking place. This is a very good way to make you aware of the difficulties some mentally ill sufferers face.

In conclusion, then, I don't think it matters whether you admit to hearing God or not to your doctor; they are fully trained to spot symptoms and signs of severe illness and doctors are not going to hospitalise you for a normal spiritual experience.

12: Psychiatry and Psychiatrists

While I was working as a staff grade psychiatrist when I was asked what I did for a living on social occasions I used to hear comments such as 'I'd better be careful what I say' or 'I expect you're analysing all of us'. I even heard 'so you can read my mind'! In fact this is far from the truth. A psychiatrist or psychologist does not continue working in every situation, and furthermore I was no better at analysing anyone at a party than any ordinary member of the public was. Certainly no one can read your mind; probably the closest you will ever get to that is when a spouse or intimate family member knows you so well that their guesses at what you are thinking are sometimes spot on!

All psychiatrists are medically qualified doctors who have specialised in the branch of medicine known as psychiatry. If the psychiatrist is a consultant, they will have taken and passed an examination known as MRCPsych, which enables him/her to become a member of the Royal College of Psychiatrists. In addition they will have had extensive training as a junior doctor and may well have additional qualifications.

They are different from psychologists, whose training does not involve a medical degree but rather qualifications in psychology. A clinical psychologist is the name given to a psychologist who is trained to work with patients and may be employed in any branch of medicine where it is appropriate to have such input. For instance, they are often used in pain clinics and neurology. In the mental health setting, they often carry out CBT (cognitive behaviour therapy).

Counsellors and Psychotherapists

Psychotherapists will have a relevant background degree, but will also have had training in their particular form of psychotherapy, such as psychodynamic psychotherapy or person centred psychotherapy; although it has to be said that there are a number of practitioners (not employed within the NHS) who have done rather less than others. Counsellors should also have done a relevant training course. The government is bringing in legislation to form a register of qualified counsellors and psychotherapists, as at the moment there is nothing to stop people from claiming to be one. So it is essential to see whether a private practitioner is registered with the BACP (British Association of Counsellors and Psychotherapists) or the ACC (Association of Christian Counsellors). Some doctors go on special training courses to become psychotherapists as well as having their medical degree and some doctors and nurses practice CBT. For most psychotherapists or counsellors, the sessions a client will have with them will be totally confidential and, though the contents of the session may be shared with their supervisor, the identity of the client is kept secret. It is always worth asking questions regarding confidentiality, although it is likely to be discussed at the very first meeting anyway.

CPN

CPNs are Community Psychiatric Nurses and they will have trained in mental health nursing, but are currently working in the community. They are an invaluable resource to the mental health team, as they often spend the most time with patients in their homes.

Social Workers

Social workers also make up part of the mental health team and will have received special training in the mental health aspects of social work, but they are not medically qualified. They do, however, also work with patients at home, and are often involved with the detention of patients when they are trained to become 'approved social workers'.

The Role of the Psychiatrist and Sectioning

Psychiatrists, like all doctors, are trained to diagnose their patients' illnesses, to treat them and to provide ongoing treatment for mental disorders, known as 'management', as necessary. They do this by talking to patients – assessing them, investigating possible causes for their conditions and excluding physical causes for the patients' illness; they prescribe drugs where needed, ECT and talking therapies, and they can refer patients onto specialist centres like the Advanced Intervention Service where I was treated under Professor Matthews in Dundee. They will be looking to collaborate with the patient's wishes as far as is possible, but they do have the powers to detain and treat patients without their consent. This may sound 'scary', but there are safeguards in place, which mean that patients and relatives can appeal against a decision and detention is in fact done only as a last resort when all attempts to persuade the patient to be admitted have failed. Subsequently the psychiatrist will use every opportunity to secure the patient's cooperation and to treat them on a voluntary basis.

The use of the power to detain and treat patients is based upon the fact that during some mental illness, the patient may lose insight into their condition and be unaware of how ill they are or whether they are ill at all. Sometimes it is necessary for the psychiatrist to detain a patient just for a number of days in order to assess them, to decide whether or not a psychiatric condition exists, but there has to be a reasonable suspicion that it does and this is a decision not based upon one doctor's opinion alone but alongside another trained mental health professional. Under the mental health act, you can only be treated against your will for the mental disorder; for instance, if you were to refuse treatment for an overdose, it cannot be given to you, but, at the same time, you could be detained in hospital for your mental condition. If this were to occur, all attempts at persuasion would be undergone to allow treatment for the overdose and to prevent an involuntary admission to hospital.

In England, Wales and Northern Ireland, these powers are known as 'sections' (in Scotland they are known as detentions) and I have been 'sectioned' on a number of occasions. I have also, as a doctor, been a signatory to allow patients to be detained under the mental health act.

When I was a doctor working in A&E, a young woman came to our department convinced that people were watching her. She was terrified that someone was going to do her some harm and no amount of reassurance would convince her otherwise. She had never been in this state before and had come to us for protection. She was shivering and shaking with fear, looking suspiciously at everything, with her eyes wide open and her pupils dilated. However she was soon convinced that even our hospital could not protect her from the prying eyes and we had to close the curtains of the room I was seeing her in, to give her sufficient peace of mind to be able to talk to me. She was greatly agitated and frightened at what was happening to her and I had to win her trust to give her a tablet to calm her down. There was one point that she thought the tablet I was giving her was poisonous and that I was colluding with her 'imagined' assailants. I say imagined, but in fact this experience was as real to her as you reading this book is to you. I decided that I needed to get a psychiatric opinion for her and that in all probability this young woman was going to need to come into hospital for treatment.

The consultant psychiatrist agreed, but the young patient did not think she was ill, she was just under attack; she thought that she had no need for hospital, just for protection. So it became necessary for her to be detained. This need was confirmed as we waited for the ambulance to take her to the local psychiatric hospital. Her fear became so overwhelming that she thought the nurse who was sitting with her and reassuring her was suddenly going to stab her; she went mad at him, grabbed a picture off the wall and attacked him. She became so violent that the police had to be called to hold her down as she lashed out at anyone and everyone.

It turned out that she had been smoking a great deal of cannabis and this was found to be the cause of this episode of 'psychosis'. She told the staff in the hospital later, when she had been treated and recovered all her faculties, that she was convinced that the police were going to chop off her arms and legs. She had been absolutely petrified. She went on to make a full recovery and was very grateful for the treatment she received and vowed she would never touch cannabis again.

This is a less than usual reaction to cannabis, but not unknown. However the reason I am telling you about it, is that it had happened to an ordinary woman but is an example of the sort of reasons that may lead to a person being sectioned!

I was sectioned for a different reason, but I also had lost insight into my condition. It was because I was so convinced of the need to commit suicide that I was detained for my own protection. You could say well why did you tell your CPN that you were going to kill yourself that day? The answer is I don't know, except that I was very upset and distressed. I wasn't looking forward to it, I was anxious and frightened and felt terribly guilty, but committing suicide seemed the reasonable thing to do. My CPN was someone I trusted and she had been specifically trained to say the right things and ask the right questions so that I confided in her.

Once in hospital, my feelings did not change and I just became more and more convinced that suicide was the answer and I wasn't willing to have ECT to treat the very serious depression that was overwhelming me. With another consultant's opinion as well as my own consultant psychiatrist, it was decided that I had to have ECT. I didn't need to be dragged to have it kicking and screaming as you may imagine, I was quite cooperative, but I hadn't consented. Fortunately this treatment lifted my depression to some extent and my acutely suicidal feelings abated. Soon after this I agreed for the need for me to be in hospital and I returned to a voluntary status. However I continued to face these kinds of dilemmas and became so unwell again before I had my neurosurgery that I continued to be under section in hospital. When I made my fantastic recovery after God healed me, before I was formally discharged from hospital, the section was lifted.

Do I regret that I was treated against my will? The answer is no. It saved my life, so even though my rights were denied it was perfectly valid. The neurosurgery I had was carried out with my full consent and in fact cannot be carried out against anyone's will. The safeguard to this is that there is a special commission who talk not only to you the patient, but also to your family and staff to make sure that you are truly consenting and have not been coerced in any way.

Negative Opinions

Not everyone is so grateful for treatment and there are a number of powerful voices who belong to the 'anti-psychiatry' movement. On many of the mental health websites, especially those which have forums to 'chat', I have come across people who are against psychiatry and medical intervention. Many of these seem to think that we are 'medicalising' normal experience or that society is defining mental illness by not accepting what we think of as abnormal behaviour as 'normal'. There are others convinced that drugs are harmful, sedate your normal self or suppress your personality. The great irony is that depression can change your personality; it certainly did mine while I was ill!

ECT is often seen as barbaric, so you can only guess what the thoughts are as to neurosurgery or other interventions. In fact there are still psychiatrists that don't accept that neurosurgery can help; I can only take it that they haven't in fact read the research relating to this matter! Often this sort of dissent is driven by personal experience of having a 'bad time' or knowing someone who has had a 'bad time'. It is essential therefore that psychiatry, in the entirety of the speciality, needs to be very careful how it treats patients, especially within hospitals. It is one of the reasons why I write about my experience because the voices of patients need to be heard in order to bring about change in these necessary institutions.

The trouble with such 'anti-psychiatry' views is that, whilst they may contain a nugget of truth, their full blown attack on psychiatry, which is often aggressive, may rub off on sufferers who could be greatly helped by their doctors and often leads to suspicion and scepticism. They have thrown the baby out with the bathwater, in my opinion.

I have been very fortunate with the vast majority of staff I have come across, but there are always 'bad apples' amongst the good, in every walk of life – it's just that those of us with mental health problems can become extremely vulnerable while we are ill and therefore are open to abuse. Because of the stigma of admitting that you may have a problem, let alone admitting that you have been in hospital, few are willing to complain. I have been told that I am very brave in speaking out. Together let's do our best to extinguish the fire that silently burns in society and in our churches. We need to set an example to the world.

13: The Diagnoses of Mental Illness: Mental Health Conditions

Mental health conditions are classified in different ways. Detailed descriptions of the different diagnoses are found in the American DSM (Diagnostic and Statistical Manual) and there is the ICD -10 (International Classification of Diseases). Both of these are used within psychiatry to make a precise diagnosis. Below is a general list of mental illnesses.

- disorders of mood
- anxiety disorders
- OCD (obsessive-compulsive disorder)
- schizophrenia and psychoses
- alcoholism and the addictions
- anorexia and bulimia
- personality disorders
- autism
- dementia

This is by no means a comprehensive list of the illnesses which are classified as psychiatric disorders or mental health conditions. Indeed some of you may be surprised to see that addictions and alcoholism are included here, but they are treated by psychiatrists as well as by specific 'agencies' who provide clinics and residential facilities and by other groups such as AA (alcoholics anonymous) and NA (narcotics anonymous). I am going to discuss each of the disorders briefly but will not do so in great detail as I want to keep this general and readable. I would expect that if you yourself are suffering or someone close to you is suffering from one of these illnesses you will have some information already and, if not, the internet can provide you with no end of detail for what you are dealing with.

You may want to know how you as a lay person can judge whether or not someone is mentally ill or not. The answer is with difficulty! You can make an informed guess if your friend or family member is behaving in a way which is uncharacteristic for them and if they are distressed or disturbed in some way. It is important not to be secretive and, if you are worried, it is better not to be talking behind the person's back but rather involve them in the conversation and even suggest in as sensitive way as possible that they might like to go and visit their GP.

I have come across various situations over the years in which individuals have looked on the internet and diagnosed another from the descriptions they have seen – this is particularly dangerous within a church setting and anyone doing such a thing should know that it is not their job to do so. This can lead to unnecessary suffering and division in the church. The sensible thing to do if you are 'labelled' with a disorder by someone who is not your doctor is to go and check it out with your GP. Even doctors can get their diagnoses wrong, so how much more so can the lay public!

Disorders of Mood

These consist of the various types of depression and bipolar disorder, which used to be called 'manic depression'.

Obviously a great deal of this book has been devoted to my own personal story of my experience with depression. In general the depressive disorders are characterised by a 'significant and pervasive lowering of mood, which is

149

inappropriate to the circumstances and usually accompanied by abnormalities in thinking, perception, bodily functions and behaviour'. What does this official description actually mean?

Firstly the lowering of mood is different from normal sadness and although it may be triggered by a sad event, such as the loss of a job or the death of a pet, it persists for longer than it should do or becomes out of proportion to the sad event. In the case of a bereavement, sadness that persists for more than six months without let up can be due to depression (though not always). On the other hand there may not be a particular trigger. Many people will look for one and it is more common to find a negative event that can be 'blamed', but the reality is that the low mood would not be sustained for such a long time. Alongside this comes a lack of enjoyment, the person finds little pleasure in life and may lose interest in things that they were formally interested in. They will usually be tired and lack energy – this can occur to such a degree that they actually slow down; they talk and move more slowly. I demonstrated this in a very marked way when I was severely ill. Apparently when I was asked a question it took me so long to answer, because my thinking had slowed up so much, that often it was thought that I hadn't heard the question or that I hadn't understood it at all.

Other symptoms also occur, such as sleeping difficulties, lack of appetite or comfort eating, with a loss or gain in weight and poor libido. Concentration may become difficult and the sufferer may also have memory difficulties. Thoughts become negative and pessimistic and may include guilty thoughts and those confirming poor self esteem. In some cases suicidal thoughts arise as do thoughts of self harm with or without actual acting out of self harm in various ways. Ultimately the illness can kill the sufferer by the intentional act of suicide. To me it is an anathema to say someone 'killed themselves' because, although there may be an element of choice, it is due to the fact that the mind is so unwell that this seems to be the only way out to a sufferer when they are severely depressed. It is certainly no act of cowardice and, although the death can be seen as extremely selfish, the depressed person who commits suicide is very unwell and will not be seeing the world from a non-depressed point of view. They may in fact feel that they are doing others good by ridding them of their 'awful' presence.

As the survivor of serious attempts on my life, I know that my thoughts were driven, almost, it seemed, externally towards these vicious desires to end my life, thinking that Phil would be able to marry a better wife and that I would rid my children of an utterly detestable mother. However, I think that, on each occasion, I wished for release from my prison, which is ultimately what happened, so I am grateful that I was so disorganised in my attempts and that the hospitals where I ended up as a result of overdosing had the skill to save me from myself. I am also most grateful that I never had the courage to carry out the more violent methods of suicide, which are sadly more often carried out by men.

Bipolar disorder has both depressive phases and manic phases. There is often, but not exclusively, a family history of this disorder in the sufferer's background.

The patient may become manic or hypomanic – basically hypomanic is a lesser degree of mania. With mania there is an elevation of mood rather than a lowering, leading to elation or excitement. The patient will have more energy and activity and will feel very well in themselves. Often s/he will become more sociable than usual, more talkative, talk faster than normal and be over familiar. They can have increased sexual energy and this may lead to promiscuity. They may not need to sleep as much and can be very irritable. Their self esteem becomes high, which can lead to belief that they are overly important, and they will also become over optimistic. Accompanying this they may become extravagant, spending money they don't have, but also can become aggressive or overly amorous or facetious. With increasing mania, the sufferer may well become irritable and suspicious rather than elated.

In a recent series on bipolar disorder featuring Stephen Fry, he asked sufferers whether they would rather do without their disease or not. His findings showed that many so enjoy the experience of being hypomanic that they would keep it. Being hypomanic often gives a tremendous energy boost to the creative sides of the personality, but unfortunately there is no guarantee that this will happen. Many people suffer tremendously with bipolar disorder, which can have a high suicidal risk.

Anxiety Disorders

We are told not to become anxious in the Bible, famously in Matthew 6:25–34:

> *Therefore I tell you, do not worry about your life, what you will eat or drink; or about your body, what you will wear. Is not life more important than food, and the body more important than clothes? Look at the birds of the air; they do not sow or reap or store away in barns and yet your heavenly Father feeds them. Are you not much more valuable that they? Can any one of you by worrying add a single hour to your life?*

This is all for good reason – we all know what it is to worry! It is unpleasant at the best of times and is singularly unproductive, yet we all do it. Imagine then what this is like when you suffer with generalised anxiety disorder – here the worry and fear is persistent, as are feelings of apprehension, irritability and being on the alert. These are often accompanied by physical symptoms, which are only useful if you literally have to run away from a situation – increased heart rate, breathlessness, sweating, dry mouth and in addition there can be tremulousness, nausea, diarrhoea, muscular tension and fatigue.

Some people develop panic attacks, during which time they are overwhelmed with symptoms of anxiety and fear, including the fear of death; they breathe too fast, which may lead to fainting or to tingling round the mouth and spasms in the hands. If you know someone is having a panic attack, it may help to give them a paper bag to breathe in and out of for five minutes, making sure that it covers the mouth and nose. Being calm and reassuring is also very helpful.

PTSD, or post traumatic stress disorder, is also one of the anxiety disorders, but is accompanied by memories and flashbacks of the traumatic event, nightmares, symptoms of anxiety, being 'hypervigilant' (on the lookout), sleep disturbance and irritability.

All of these conditions are treatable, usually by a combination of drugs and cognitive behaviour therapy.

OCD

OCD is obsessive-compulsive disorder. This can reach a very serious degree, so much so that the sufferer's whole life may be taken up with the disorder and they may become severely disabled. In the most extreme forms it can be treated with the same kind of operation that I had for my severe depression, with the same criteria – namely that the patient has to have tried every other kind of treatment.

An obsession is a thought, impulse or image which is highly resisted, recurrent, persistent, intrusive and unpleasant. For instance, an obsession may be that everything is dirty or contaminated and may be followed by a compulsion such as repetitive hand washing, cleaning or opening doors using a handkerchief, wiping down seats before sitting in them etc. Another obsession may be to do with doubt, leading to the compulsion of needing to check everything repetitively – there is usually an accompanying thought that something dreadful will happen if the person fails to carry out the compulsion.

Also quite commonly obsessions may have a highly sexual content, which must be extremely distressing for the individual sufferer. Remember, these thoughts or images are unwanted, the person tries to resist them, but they are repetitive and recurrent and intrude in on that person. In other words they are quite outside the person's control. I am sure, though, that the sufferer will inevitably feel responsible and therefore guilty and probably full of sin, even though this is not their fault.

OCD is a serious disorder that, if not treated, may lead to alcohol or drug abuse because the sufferer gets no respite; they can also become depressed and they may commit suicide.

Schizophrenia and Other Psychoses

Everyone has heard of schizophrenia, but a good many people misunderstand what this means. One thing I must clear up right from the start – it does *not* mean split personality!

It is relatively common and occurs throughout the world. It is a mixture of symptoms and signs 'characterised by disturbances in thinking and communications, with delusions and hallucinations, set against a background of gradual cognitive decline as well as social deterioration.'

Psychiatrists further classify schizophrenia and paranoid schizophrenia, which, although well known, is simply one of the sub-types.

A delusion is a falsely held belief that is not in keeping with the patients' social and cultural norms or values. The patient cannot be persuaded out of it and firmly holds the belief to be true. An example of this is a delusion of guilt – the patient believes that they are responsible and culpable for the event/situation/occurrence even when this is manifestly incorrect.

A hallucination is a sensory perception which is not created by an external stimulus, such as 'voices' that are actually heard even though no physical sound has created the voice. It can also take the form of visions, such as seeing something or someone who is not there in reality, but will be totally real to the sufferer. (This is unlike a Christian seeing a vision, where they know that what they see is in fact a vision.)

So a person with schizophrenia who thinks that she is the queen will actually believe this, despite the fact that she is not living in a palace. She may well expect others to treat her as a royal person despite the fact that she is not in any way dressed like a royal and may even be in dishevelled clothing and surroundings. She cannot be persuaded out of it even if presented with all the facts.

Hallucinations and delusions are what are called psychotic symptoms and don't just occur in schizophrenia but also in severe depression, mania and other conditions. It is quite possible to have a single episode of schizophrenia and completely recover – as indeed it is for other psychotic illnesses. I described the young woman with a psychotic illness as a result of smoking cannabis in an earlier chapter. However, for the majority of cases, schizophrenia is a life long illness and it really would take a miracle for someone to totally recover. As it is there are drugs called antipsychotics, which control most of the symptoms, but even the newer drugs, which are more tolerable in terms of side effects, do nothing to stop the decline in cognitive ability and socialisation that some afflicted individuals suffer. It is a horrible, horrible illness and most sufferers have to be cared for outside the home, as the high emotion which inevitably arises in a family situation can lead to relapse. But there is increasing evidence that if some sufferers with schizophrenia are allowed, and are able, to manage their own illnesses, then they can live a normal, highly productive life, despite their disability.

Alcoholism and the Addictions

People who become alcoholics are looked down upon in society. They are thought of as those who have 'given in', and seen to be weak in character and morally questionable. The facts are that alcohol is an addictive substance and becoming addicted happens readily for some more than others; upbringing and genetics play a part. Biblically there is no reason why you and I cannot have a drink; however drinking to excess or getting drunk is not part of God's plan. Yet while the description 'alcoholic' is seen as a derogatory term, many ordinary people see drinking and getting drunk as a game we can play and enjoy. Such is the hypocrisy amongst our society. Many who do become alcoholics use alcohol to relieve the stresses and strains in their lives or use it to self medicate for physical as well as mental pain. It is really important not to judge these people who have succumbed to such an addiction.

Sometimes hospitalisation or admission to a residential unit is needed for the alcoholic to 'dry out'. This is because there is not only a mental dependence to alcohol, but also a physical dependence and it can be very dangerous to suddenly stop the alcohol; this may lead to fitting, brain damage and even death. Once the withdrawal or detoxification is complete with the help of appropriate medication, a satisfactory outcome is achieved as far as the physical dependence is concerned, but the mental dependence is much harder to overcome and often leads to relapse. All the talking therapies and AA or similar support groups can be successful in overcoming this addiction, but for a friend or family member often much patience and a positive, caring attitude is needed.

Most of us are addicted to something. There is not such an outcry when the addictive substance is food or nicotine. Cigarette smoking does not get the same judgement from society as other addictions do, even though it is becoming less socially acceptable now. As for food, we dare not raise our voices because there is so much obesity around, yet dependence on food as a comfort, or eating in response to stress or boredom, is very clearly happening all around us. The saying 'I only have to look at a lettuce leaf to put on weight' is untrue. You cannot put on weight unless you eat more than your body requires, although we are meant to come in different shapes and sizes. However it is true also that some drugs change the appetite so that you eat more and this is very commonly the case if you are on medication for a mental health condition. But, as we all know from the media, as a society we need to eat less and exercise more. For some, tackling their weight loss means overcoming their 'addiction' to food. (It is not a true addiction, because food is necessary to the body, but in other ways if fulfils the criteria.)

Addictions to drugs are another source of society's judgemental attitude. This is seen because most addicts came into contact with drugs during their youth, by the way of experimentation. Drug addicts are seen as criminals, the dregs of society, the lowest of the low, so imagine where Jesus would be – sitting amongst them no doubt. Not everyone is addicted to illicit drugs; there are also plenty of addicts amongst the normal population addicted to pain killers or to other drugs especially of the class which the well known valium is a member of. These drugs are called the benzodiazepines and doctors are reluctant to prescribe them long term by reason of their potential for addiction, however they can be useful in the short term for various conditions.

Most people who are addicted to any substance will have two problems – the physical addiction and the psychological addiction. The physical addiction can be dealt with by gradual withdrawal of the substance possibly using medication to make this easier; it is the mental addiction that invariably causes the most problems. As an addict, you need to face the reason you are using that substance; look at why you may have the need to be 'propped up' – is it because you are unable to face work, to cope with stress, is there constant conflict in your life etc? But it will also be difficult to give up for the simple reason that the effects of the addicted substance are invariably pleasurable.

A lot of the addiction clinics in the mental health setting are looking at drug addicted individuals who may have other mental health conditions as well or require drug replacement therapy. I believe for Christians we can become free, we are called to be free in fact, but once again this may take time and a lot of patience – with much support in prayer and in friendship. Of course there are the exceptions such as those described in Jackie Pullinger's book *Chasing the Dragon*, a true story of miracle after miracle as addicts in Hong Kong came off heroin without even experiencing cold turkey when those around prayed in tongues. Wouldn't it be great if we could hear of such testimonies coming from the UK too?

Anorexia and Bulimia

Anorexia nervosa is a condition known to many. It involves a morbid fear of fatness, with excessive dieting and exercising to produce a state similar to starvation. It can be extremely dangerous and coexist with other mental health conditions.

Many of the physical organ systems are affected and in girls this will mean a shutting down of the production of female sex hormones, so amenorrhea (lack of periods) is the result. This condition is not exclusive to girls, although the ratio is one male to ten females. It must be all the more painful for a boy with this condition since it is seen as a female disease.

It is inevitably distressing for the families concerned as well as the sufferer and much more so if the condition is so severe that s/he needs hospitalisation. There are no drugs that can cure the condition, although drugs are often used to help with depression or obsessions which may accompany the disorder. Cognitive behaviour therapy and sometimes family therapy have been found to be helpful in some cases.

There was a time when the parents, especially the father, were thought to be the cause of this condition but that is not born out in practice. However it can leave a legacy of guilt in the family. It is good when a church can stand in support of affected families as well as the individual concerned.

Bulimia is a less severe condition but nonetheless is important. This occurs in a ratio of 50:1 females to males. Usually the young woman is normal or overweight but has periods of eating excessively, bingeing, followed by self induced vomiting or purging with laxatives. She has a basic problem with impulse control and will have a very low self esteem. She feels guilty that she is behaving in this way but seems unable to stop it. She also may be suffering from depression, OCD, personality disorder or other psychiatric disorders. This condition may be amenable to drug treatment as well as some of the talking therapies.

Personality Disorders

Until recently personality disorders were felt to be untreatable, but, with appropriate psychotherapy, the deeply ingrained patterns of behaviour that are termed 'maladaptive' may be reversed, and it is good that more flexible patterns of response may be gained.

All of us have personality traits or characteristics but they are flexible and adaptive; in a personality disorder they are fixed, unhelpful and may cause the person distress or impair their social functioning. Often people diagnosed with personality disorders have come from dysfunctional family backgrounds and some may have been abused. A personality disorder can result if this is a child's experience within the first five years of his/her life.

There are a number of different types of personality disorder described and I will not go into detail except for one that is termed 'borderline personality disorder', as it confuses people. The name does not refer to the disorder being borderline. In fact I do not know why this disorder has the word borderline attached to it at all.

Afflicted people are prone to mood instability, have a poor self image and tend to be impulsive. They have a pervasive feeling of emptiness, even boredom, yet are 'emotionally charged'. They tend to have unstable relationships characterised by a fear of abandonment and may well indulge in repeated acts of self harm or suicidal behaviour. These individuals are prone to depression and also may drift into drug or alcohol abuse. Within the Church, or other social organisations, these people will find it difficult to maintain relationships, will be constantly falling out with others and are often seen as manipulative. They will constantly be 'needy' and there will be little progress in terms of true spiritual growth. It can be most frustrating to deal with them and will be difficult when self harm is involved, but, like anyone, the person with a personality disorder is deserving of our love and forgiveness. They may well have faced a background of constant rejection so it is important not to reject them even if they reject you. Boundary setting may well be necessary, with the proviso that broken boundaries will lead to firm but loving correction given with understanding concern, not a punitive attitude.

A Quick Mention of Autism

Autism spectrum disorders is the proper name for this condition. It can be highly variable in how it appears in any one individual. It is a neurodevelopmental disease and manifests as difficulty in communication and social interaction, restricted interests and repetitive behaviour. It varies greatly in how it affects people; some are totally disabled even without speech, but for others it is barely noticeable. This condition includes asperger's syndrome.

In one of the churches where we were members there was a family whose little boy was diagnosed with autism. He was seen to be extremely 'disruptive' and 'badly behaved' at times and the family suffered a great deal of stress as a result. It just reminds me how careful we must be in our judgement of others. Obviously the situation may happen that there is a lack of discipline within a family but we must not be quick to criticise; rather we should try to support and understand where the family is at. This particular little boy needed a diagnosis to explain to his worried parents just why he wasn't responding in a normal way to the process of socialisation and to play and needed expert help with his growing up process.

Dementia

Many families are seeing the awful scourge of the dementias – alzheimer's, lewy–body dementia or multi-infarct dementia, which is effectively dementia caused by mini strokes. These diseases usually affect the elderly, but not always, and they cause terrible suffering in particular for those caring for an affected person. Of course in the early course of the disease, to be given this diagnosis must be absolutely devastating to the sufferer, but as the disease progresses they will lose the memory and the insight into the illness.

I have a friend who I met in Dundee who has the very grave diagnosis of Huntingdon's disease; this is a type of dementia that affects the young. There is a movement disorder as well as the deterioration in cognitive functions of memory, attention, language and problem solving. This disease is genetic and usually 50 per cent of the children of an affected parent will have inherited the particular gene that is responsible for this condition. The symptoms usually start in midlife and Caroline showed signs of the movement disorder before she reached her 40th birthday. She knew from the age of 28 that she was going to suffer with this devastating disease and that ultimately it would cause her death. She is tremendously brave and I am sure all your hearts will go out to her as mine has done and pray that her suffering won't be too hard to bear for herself, her family and for her very close and faithful friends.

I watched from a distance as my father-in-law suffered with multi-infarct dementia. With this there is a steep, marked deterioration rather than a gradual deterioration, so he never knew about his condition to the best of our knowledge. The first thing that alerted us to his condition was at Christmas when he didn't know what to do with a present. He just kept staring at it, turning it over again and again. It soon became evident that there was something very wrong going on. Because the short term memory is one of the first things 'to go', it was not noticeable to anyone outside the family that anything was wrong; he appeared to give straight forward and correct information to his GP, saying everything was fine when in fact it was anything but correct! As his memory deteriorated, he did what many sufferers do – that is to confabulate. They don't know that they are doing it, but are literally making up stories to deal with the loss of facts that the memory would normally provide. This did not last for long for Douglas – he lost his independence quite rapidly and his loving wife soon became his full time carer. When he was in hospital for what turned out to be his last illness, Thelma his wife needed to be with him as any time he needed anything or felt uncomfortable, he wasn't able to summon a nurse – if he remembered to ring the bell, he certainly did not remember why he had done so. Sadly, the night he died Thelma had been told to leave by the night staff and his sudden deterioration was unnoticed by the staff and he died alone.

These illnesses are most distressing for family and friends to witness. The husband or wife may literally lose their other half bit by bit and yet the dementia sufferer's physical presence is there and may be in relative good health for quite some time. However they may require round the clock attention and not manage ordinary activities of daily living such as toileting or washing. Often the difficult decision may have to be reached that they can no longer be cared for at home, which leaves the family members caught in the turmoil of guilt and relief. There are many devoted carers and they themselves need to be supported as often outings like shopping become extremely difficult to organise and their own needs become neglected. The personal stress they face is enormous but often they will not show it, rather they wear a smile as they weather through the storm of their ordeal.

The same is true for carers of any sufferer of a mental health condition, especially if the sufferer is a spouse or family member. There is a forgotten army out there doing their best to care for someone who, through no fault of their own, may be very difficult and challenging to look after. When my depression was at its most severe stage, Phil cared not only for me but also for our four children at home as well as having a full time job. Thankfully he had help from our parents, and the friendship and assistance from various other people, but at no time was he offered counselling or support by the mental health services who were so involved with me. Praise God that our church friends were so supportive, but he was rarely able to open himself up even to them; this was partly because he was responsible for his family and therefore felt the need to hold it all together. Most of the time he acted as an automaton with his trust in God, but without the opportunity to express his own needs. Our loving heavenly Father is so gracious that, all in good time, Phil has been relieved of his tremendous burden and our whole family has come to terms with the ordeal we all had to face.

14: Treatments and Therapies

The aim of this chapter is to describe the range of treatments that are available for those who have mental disorders, rather than specifically naming drugs and dosages. It is also not an exhaustive list. I have experienced most of the treatments available for severe depression, but by no means all of them and my views are entirely personal – I am not speaking for the medical profession as a whole. I am not giving much space for self help, which is widely available for milder conditions and for which there are many different approaches.

Drug Treatment

Many disorders are treated with drugs. Some people are wary of taking drugs for mental disorders, mostly because of misinformation and fear of the long term effects. I have heard people in Christian circles say that it is wrong to take medicines for psychological disorders. I would ask the same people whether or not it is right to take medicine for high blood pressure. Mental illness is no different, in that it is an illness that needs treatment. It is true that some disorders do need to be treated for life, such as chronic schizophrenia, but also for those like me who have had recurrent severe depression. In these contexts the drugs are often prescribed to prevent relapse rather than to treat symptoms.

Antidepressants

Antidepressants are given to relieve the symptoms of depression (and some anxiety disorders), by speeding up the natural remission of the illness and for preventing relapse. They affect the levels of various neurotransmitters (chemical messengers) in the brain. Some antidepressants are also given for pain relief in certain disorders.

Antidepressants are not addictive. It is true that for a lot of these drugs the patient has to come off them slowly, but this is to avoid unpleasant withdrawal effects. Also there are different 'classes' of antidepressants and some of these are not compatible with each other, so it is perfectly possible that a patient may need a gap after finishing one drug before starting the next.

Antidepressants are not 'happy pills'. If you are not suffering from depression, they won't have an effect other than side effects. They help your low mood to come up, but they won't make you happy. Only you and the Lord can do that. Happiness is more often than not related to contentment, and we know, as Paul says, that it is something to be learned: 'for I have learned to be content whatever the circumstances'. Philippians 4:11 TNIV

The newer drugs are much safer in overdose and you can become quite tolerant to the side effects, so they are often preferred by the patient and doctor alike. However the older drugs are still used in some contexts, especially in cases of 'difficult to treat depression'.

I have experienced a large number of different antidepressants during my illnesses and have always felt that they are worth taking despite the side effects. My depression was such that even if the medication relieved a small amount of my symptoms, it would be worthwhile. However it is no good if the treatment makes you feel worse than the illness itself – although clearly that is not a general assumption as chemotherapy for cancer would rarely be taken if that were the case.

Like most drugs, antidepressants must be taken regularly to work and it is a good idea to get into a routine. I have a glass of water by my bed, so I take my medication when I go to bed and when I get up. Fortunately, this way, I rarely forget to take them. Other people link them to having meals, but remember, whatever you do, as for any regularly prescribed drug it is important to keep taking them. If a problem arises, then an appointment should be made with your GP, rather than just stopping the medication. If the problem is urgent, ask for an urgent appointment.

Many people stop antidepressants too early – once they feel well, they 'don't see the point' in continuing to take them, but crucially they are also needed for relapse prevention. The risk of relapse is greatest during the first six months after a depressive episode, so it would seem wise to continue the drug during this time. There is a maxim in the medical world for antidepressants: 'what gets you well, keeps you well'.

Sometimes other drugs are prescribed with the antidepressants to make their effects greater, so it is possible to be on quite a few medications – although for most depression which is treated by the GP that is not the case.

Drugs for Anxiety

There are generally three sorts of drugs used for anxiety, those for the physical symptoms alone, known as beta-blockers, those which affect the brain like antidepressants do and those which cause relaxation. The drugs that are given to promote relaxation are usually given on a short term basis only as the benzodiazepines like diazepam are addictive.

Anxiety disorders are more often treated with a combination of drug treatment and talking therapies.

Antipsychotics

These are drugs used to relieve the symptoms of psychosis, like hallucinations (voices, visions etc) and delusions. They are also used to boost the response of an antidepressant. They can be given as tablets or injections. The depot injection is useful for sufferers on long term treatment as they can have all their medication for 3–4 months in one single injection. These medicines often cause the patient to put on weight.

Lithium and Anticonvulsants

Lithium is commonly used in bipolar disorder but so are anticonvulsants – drugs for the treatment of epilepsy, because they are 'mood stabilisers'. They are also used in recurrent depression. Lithium is a drug that needs its blood levels monitoring because if it is too low, it won't be effective. Too high, and it can be toxic. However it is highly effective and has transformed the lives of many sufferers.

Sleeping Tablets

These are regularly used for patients with mental disorders because sleep is often disrupted in a major way. Doctors are reluctant to prescribe them for long periods as it is easy to become dependent on them; I had quite a lot of difficulty sleeping without them after my healing, but eventually overcame this problem.

Talking Therapies

NICE, the National Institute for Clinical Excellence, has produced guidelines for the treatment of many diseases, disorders and conditions. Mental health is no exception. A lot of the more common mental illnesses like anxiety and depression have talking therapies given as the first line treatment by NICE, but the truth is that they are not as readily available as doctors would like so often they resort to drug treatment first, particularly if the waiting lists are long.

There are many different kinds of counselling and psychotherapy, some of which are available on the NHS and some that are private. Some of the private centres are run on a means tested basis, so can still be affordable for those on low incomes.

NICE specifically mentions the use of Cognitive Behaviour Therapies, as it has been the most researched therapy and has been found to be effective in the treatment of anxiety disorders and depression. I have received both CBT and other forms of psychotherapy and counselling. In my experience the really essential thing is that you get on well with the therapist and you feel you can trust them and build a rapport with them. I do not deny the value of CBT, but am wary of very short courses and I still think you need to interact well with the therapist however long you see them for.

At the present time there are no regulations in place to prevent anyone from calling themselves a psychotherapist or counsellor, so it is always necessary to find out what sort of training people have had. There are associations which therapists may join, the most notable being the BACP (British

Association of Counsellors and Psychotherapists) and the ACC (Association of Christian Counsellors). I think it is often reassuring for a Christian to go for counselling to a Christian therapist as long as they have had proper training. However it is important that you find out whether or not the counsellor is a Nouthetic counsellor, who believes that the Bible exclusively contains all the answers to a person's psychological problems and therefore ignores knowledge obtained in other contexts, like psychology or psychotherapy. Their emphasis is in finding out where the root of the problem lies in terms of sin. These counsellors may also call themselves 'biblical' counsellors and their founder is Jay E. Adams. Personally I do not recommend these counsellors, as their base is very narrow.

Good psychotherapy allowed me to access my innermost being. It is as if I was a house with many rooms; naturally I could go into certain rooms, but others were shut off, with the doors closed and locked. Counselling allowed me to carefully open up those doors, so I could receive healing there. My aim is to be integrated, whole. The word *shalom* in the Bible means peace but it refers to being whole. '"For I know the plans I have for you", declares the Lord, "plans to prosper you and not to harm you, plans to give you hope and a future"' (Jeremiah 29:11). The word for hope is in fact translated from the same Hebrew word *shalom*, a hope, a peace, a wholeness. That's what I need; inner wholeness, peace and hope. Despite the fact that none of my psychotherapists were Christians, God in His graciousness has allowed me to explore my inner world and I am sure whether it be with the help of more counselling or without, I have more areas to discover. After all life is a journey, but praise God it ends in a good and perfect destination, heaven!

CBT

Cognitive Behavioural Therapy (CBT) is based on the theory of Aaron Beck. It works on the principle that emotional problems result from unhelpful thought processes and underlying personal beliefs. Counselling is seen as a collaborative process in which the counsellor and client work together to uncover these beliefs and cycles of thinking and reform them to produce a more positive emotional experience. CBT is regarded as an evidence-based system of therapy, lending itself to short term counselling, and is widely used within the NHS.

Psychodynamic Psychotherapy

Psychodynamic counselling is an approach based originally on the principles of Sigmund Freud. Psychodynamics emphasises the unconscious conflicts which occur initially during a person's childhood. The counsellor seeks to bring these thoughts and feelings to consciousness using techniques such as free association and making use of the dynamic created by the relationship between client and counsellor. The assumption is that gaining insight into these unconscious processes will in itself bring relief from them.

Person Centred Psychotherapy

Person centred counselling was developed by Carl Rogers. The technique works on the assumption that the counsellor's relationship with the client is central to bringing resolution to their problems. The counsellor works to create a comfortable environment by demonstrating empathy, congruence (genuineness) and positive self-regard, which is described as an attitude of grace and unconditional acceptance of people regardless of what they say and do. It is considered that this will lead to a process of self-actualisation; whereby the client discovers his or her own solutions.

ECT

Electroconvulsive therapy (ECT) has a long history and in its most primitive form was first known to be used by the Romans when they put a sufferer in a bath of electric eels. We have come a long way since then. It is now known that a fit or convulsion causes a release of neurotransmitters in the brain, which elevates low mood and normalises high mood in the case of mania of bipolar disorder. For this treatment to be effective a number of sessions need to be given under the supervision of a psychiatrist so that the patient's condition can be closely monitored.

The patient is fasted overnight, as for any general anaesthetic, and taken to a purpose built room where s/he lies down on a couch. There will be a minimum of a nurse specifically trained in ECT, a psychiatric doctor and anaesthetist present. The anaesthetist places a small needle into the back of the hand and administers an anaesthetic drug to put the patient to sleep. Then s/he will give a muscle relaxant before the psychiatrist uses a special machine to administer an electric current to the head, which causes the patient to fit. Because of the muscle relaxant, the only evidence of the fit will be the fluttering of the eyelids. There are no jerks as are seen in anyone fitting or in the films or TV depicting ECT before the days of anaesthetics. The patient will not be aware of anything from the time s/he has been put to sleep until the time s/he awakes.

On one occasion the anaesthetist made a mistake with me. I was given the muscle relaxant agent, which effectively paralyses you, before being put to sleep. I was absolutely terrified to be awake and about to be given the shock, but was unable to tell anyone. However, I did not feel a thing – apparently you don't feel the shock or have any memory of it. This did little to reassure me though and, for that course of ECT, I would not continue. But I must emphasise that it was the anaesthetist who was at fault. Fortunately such a problem is a rare event and I did recover my confidence and go on to have many more ECT treatments.

The side effects include a possible headache straight after the event, which can be treated with a simple painkiller, and possible loss of memory for the immediate time surrounding the ECT – this can lead to confusion. After a few hours, this disappears, but memory loss may persist and can be quite troublesome for the patient. Severe depression and mania also cause memory loss and these are the most common reason for which ECT is prescribed as a treatment; so it is never easy to ascertain whether memory loss is truly caused by the ECT or the illness itself, though undoubtedly ECT does cause memory loss.

This treatment is not proposed lightly, but it can be highly effective in returning the patient to a much better mood state and I can vouch for that. Out of the many patients I have met who received this treatment, I did not meet one who regretted it – even though most complained of some sort of memory impairment.

More Advanced Treatments

Deep Brain Stimulation: This is an experimental treatment for depression and, as far as I am aware, is only being carried out in two centres in the UK currently, although research trials are awaited and are going to take place at Ninewells Hospital in Dundee. It has been used successfully in the treatment of the motor symptoms of Parkinson's disease.

Vagus Nerve Stimulation: This is a neurosurgical treatment that consists of stimulating the vagus nerve that runs through the neck. The stimulator is much like a cardiac pacemaker and it has been successful for various individuals who have treatment refractory depression.

Neurosurgery: Anterior Cingulotomy is the name given to the operation I had. It involves placing two lesions in the anterior cingulate of the brain by stereotactic surgery; the exact area is pin pointed by using MRI and CT guidance and just this area is targeted. It is used for certain individuals who have treatment refractory depression or severe and disabling treatment-resistant obsessive-compulsive disorder (OCD), but is only offered after a review of the treatments that have been tried previously and recommendations for further treatments have been implemented.

If you want to find out more about these treatments, I refer you to the website of the Advanced Interventions Service at Dundee (www.advancedinterventions.org.uk).

15: Blessings and Curses

The mere mention of curses makes me shiver. It reminds me of the fairytale books I used to have read to me as a child, of wicked witches and ogres; but always there was a happy ending as a fairy or beautiful prince broke the curse. Therefore to believe that curses are a reality has needed more than just a vivid imagination. Blessings I can take and I want more of them. No, they are not a problem. Of course reading the Old Testament, there are plenty of mentions of curses. In Genesis 3:17, God curses the ground after Adam and Eve have eaten the forbidden fruit. Later, in Deuteronomy, Moses lays down the options of blessings or curses for the children of Israel, which they themselves could determine according to whether they followed the rules of the covenant, which include the Ten Commandments, or chose to disobey God by turning away from Him.

Curses were not just an Old Testament phenomenon though; Jesus Himself curses the fig tree which had no fruit on it (Mark 11:21). When the Romans arrested Paul on his return to Jerusalem, he was rescued from a group of men who had bound themselves with a curse to kill him (Acts 23:21). James also warns us when speaking of the tongue that we may bless the Lord and also curse men. This does not give us the full picture if we think of cursing as merely saying rude or blasphemous words, which is the essence of our modern interpretation. I had heard of modern curses, but I never thought for a moment that they would apply to me, so, when I heard of Phil's description of what went on in the prayer group before I had surgery, I was not doubtful but just a little surprised. I then read *Blessings and Curses* by Derek Prince and that made it clearer.

My Case – an Example

When the prayer group formed to pray for me, the subject of blessings and curses came up – well, to be specific, curses did. Phil told me that enquiry was made whether he knew of any curses which could have been put on me or my family. He knew of no witchcraft or other forms of the occult that could have been in my past or family background. However we have always been aware that there had been a family link to free masonry on my father's side. While this was being explored in more detail, one of the members of the team had a picture which was of a symbol unknown to him. In our church was a member who had held an elevated position in the free mason's hierarchy and Phil took it to him to interpret. Sure enough it was one of their symbols and so further prayer took place to break any curses which could have been put over me at some time in my family history.

This is not something we should be afraid of as there is power in the name of Jesus and God's power is infinitely greater than any other in the universe, including that of the enemy. He may want to hold us bound, but the Father wants us to be free and His will always prevails – the power of the curse is broken, He has the victory. Hallelujah!

But more significantly, after I received my healing and gave my testimony of the light switching on, it happened that it was the morning in our church on which Graham Cooke was preaching. Now I knew very little about Graham Cooke until Phil explained to me afterwards that his ministry concerned the prophetic. He gave his sermon and about half way through, he announced that he had a specific word for me. I tell you, my eyes lit up, God was speaking personally to me through this man of God! He told me that having lived through seven years of 'curses' (as in the Old Testament sense), God had said I would have seven years of blessing. Though there were seven years that the locust had eaten, they would be restored. I was thrilled and full of faith as a result of this prophesy. It was in line with God's word as all prophesy should be and I was to have this confirmed in other ways too.

Now this all seemed to go to plan as far as physical blessings were concerned. I regained my former fitness and figure; our household became solvent once again. Very importantly I fitted into our family once again and enjoyed the closeness of our teenage children. I returned to work where I had left off and indeed progressed with my success at exams and subsequent promotion. But where did my relapse fit in or Phil's redundancy? Well the redundancy did mean we started a new life and, though we were not as well off financially, God blessed us with all that we needed. The relapse however could not be looked on in the same light. It is true to say, that in terms of intensity, it was not anything like as bad as the first illness. I responded to treatment and I was in hospital for less than six months! Not only that but I was under the team who were most experienced at handling my condition. If we hadn't moved to Scotland, I would have had to be treated in the DOP, which I would have hated given my experience the first time round. As it was, I went back to Dundee where the team knew me and I had superb care.

But I realise looking back that the one area of my life which has certainly been blessed without a shadow of a doubt is my spiritual life. Even now when I have had the most recent down times, I am aware that my soul has remained well – the redeemed soul longs for God and I think that has always been true for me. I had grown tremendously over the seven years since my healing. Whatever has gone on in my life, my growth has been upward and I feel extremely blessed even now I am beyond the seven years – it didn't suddenly stop! I admit I am still left with questions about why I had to have the relapse and why I am not living in the situation after the initial healing – drug free and well, but I have decided that I will not be drawn into questions that cannot be answered this side of eternity. I am content with my life and trust all of my circumstances to the Lord. He deserves all my praise, whatever befalls me, like the marriage vows, for better for worse, for richer for poorer, in sickness or in health, I can thank the Lord that He has won the victory and He has the whole world in his hands! Also I am still hopeful that I will receive complete healing from the Lord, but my life does not depend on it!

The Role of Spiritual Warfare

Speaking of spiritual warfare, I think it is really important that we put on the whole armour of God: Eph 6:11, 14–17 (NASB):

Put on the full armour of God, so that you will be able to stand firm against the schemes of the devil... Stand firm therefore, having girded your loins with truth and having put on the breastplate of righteousness, and having shod your feet with the preparation of the gospel of peace; in addition to all, taking up the shield of faith with which you will be able to extinguish all the flaming arrows of the evil one. And take the helmet of salvation and the sword of the Spirit which is the word of God.

The helmet of salvation guards our minds, but other parts of the armour are just as important, and then we are called to stand, to hold our ground. It is very difficult to do this when depressed because so little of it makes sense to the mind, which is already being attacked. For sure the illness causes depressive thoughts, but I do believe that the enemy takes hold of them when at all possible and hits hard. The depression tells you that you are worthless and I can almost imagine a demon sitting there near to the person and shrieking at the top of its voice, 'that's right you are useless, always have been since the day you were born'. At first the depressed Christian may well fight back, I know I did, but with time and the other burdens like lack of sleep, low energy and feeling really unwell and miserable, I could no longer retaliate. I gave in, just accepted that that was how I was, worthless and useless; it became my truth. I needed others to take me to the feet of Jesus, like the four friends brought the paralytic, down through the roof. (Mark 2:4) I think it is good to pray over someone not just for their healing, but also for their protection, literally dressing them in the armour of God. Why? Because it is scriptural and, for sure, they will be receiving the flaming arrows of the evil one. Jesus commends the friends for their faith, so He will commend the sufferer's friends too.

Another very effective tool against the enemy is praise. The devil hates it when we praise God and he won't be found in heaven where God is praised continuously. Usually praise is very hard for the mentally ill. When I went to church and praise was sung, I found I could cope with the slower, more melodious songs or hymns, particularly when they had themes I could relate to, but outright praise involved great determination and effort if I could sing or speak at all. However being in the presence of praise and worship of the musical variety, even if I couldn't join in, often gave me a sense of peace and I could relax. When I was recovering in the Carseview Centre in Dundee, I often used to put my headphones on and just listen to a praise CD; it did far more for me than just music on its own. It brought me to tears quite often as well as relaxation and prayer. Surprisingly tears can be hard to come by when you are severely depressed and, when that is the case, they are often very releasing. I used to use the CD at night when I was trying to go off to sleep and, despite the discomfort of the earphones, I really believe it helped me to sleep better.

Back to My Story

As my recovery continued I had accepted that I was now retired from work, but this didn't mean I could never go back to work as a doctor – merely that I could not go back to the particular job that I had been doing. This helped tremendously because it meant the door was not closed if I wanted to return to A&E in the future. The professor told me that I should not start looking at work until I had been stable and stress free for more than a year. I continued on a high dose of antidepressants and was accepting that I may have to stay on them for life. It was a lot of change to my normal way of thinking, which is if there's a problem you should simply work hard until you fix it. Not always a very helpful way of approaching life, maladaptive in depression.

I did have one or two compensations though. I have been invited to speak since writing my first book, but I had one major event to look forward to. I was asked to speak to a group of student nurses, most of who were training in mental health, at Southampton University. I had been asked before but had not been able to take up the offer because it had been the time when I was in hospital, so I felt really delighted and also very privileged to be asked back a second time. The real good news about the DOP in Southampton is that they had decided to split the wards into separate male and female wards and to build a completely new centre for the patients and apparently they were listening to what I said – my book is on the recommended reading list for their student nurses.

Our time in Scotland was drawing to a close though. We had two grandchildren on the way and suddenly we seemed too far away from our children who remained in the south of England, with the exception of Jonathan who was living out in the USA.

Phil started looking for jobs in the area we had come from originally, but this time he had managerial experience within IT and the NHS, so surely it would be easier to obtain work than it had been at the time of his redundancy four years ago? It's funny how God works. The perfect job came up and Phil was interviewed but he did not get it – we were both highly disappointed and asking the question 'why' again. Well we did find out the answer. Phil's work became extremely stressful and, when he was having some time off, he started to think of what he would really like to do. Now that is not something which he did lightly – he had never had the liberty to do this before and he came to the conclusion that he would like to apply to do a Theology and Counselling degree at the London School of Theology. Remarkably this coincided with him being left some money so financially it was possible. At no time before then could we have possibly considered this course of action. We shared this with our minister and our friends and they were of one mind, that this was definitely what God wanted for us.

Before we left Banchory we were able to travel to the USA to visit our son Jonathan, who was doing a school of ministry course with Rick Joyner's church in North Carolina. As well as being a great time seeing our son, we attended a conference at the church and on one particular day they had a time when people could be prayed over for healing. I decided to go for this: there were two people there to pray for me and I told them about my depression. They laid hands on me and asked God to completely heal me. I did not feel anything at all, but I have put it into the Father's hands – I want to be completely healed, but since then I have had two minor flare ups. Maybe I will still be healed, maybe I won't, but I do believe that God is with me; He will never leave me or forsake me and I am not alone, He will never leave or forsake any of His children!

So in August 2009 we moved down to Northwood just north of London to settle near to the college. My illness was described as stable at this point, but Prof and the team did not want to reduce my medication since a move is considered a highly stressful activity, even if it was going to bring us in closer proximity to our wider family.

Our move has been successful, although I did have a downturn shortly after moving. But now we are settled in Watford Community Church and are very much enjoying our new life.

When I was preparing for one of the recent times I was to speak, the Lord gave me this to share:

There is hope for the mentally ill – we can be free in Jesus' name. We can tell the world what we have suffered from and how we've been set free by God's Holy Spirit working in our lives, revealing to us what Jesus did for us, bearing our pain when He was beaten; by His stripes we are healed! Hallelujah, hallelujah! We have an intimate caring Father who never condemns us because our sins are wiped clean by the blood of Jesus. He is wonderful. We are adopted in God's family, we are His children; we have the perfect parent who is there for us all the time, not just some of the time, all of the time, and when we are worshippers He even chooses to use us. Yes, even us, the weak, the frail, the low to confound the wise of this world, to set more people like us free.

My hope while I am here on earth is to take on the mantle described in Isaiah 61:1–3 (NASB), as I mentioned in the introduction. I think it is worth repeating:

The Spirit of the Lord God is upon me, because the Lord has anointed me to bring good news to the afflicted. He has sent me to bind up the broken hearted, to proclaim liberty to captives and freedom to prisoners; to proclaim the favourable year of the Lord and the day of vengeance of our God; to comfort all who mourn, to grant those who mourn in Zion, giving them a garland instead of ashes, the oil of gladness instead of mourning. The mantle of praise instead of a spirit of fainting, so they will be called oaks of righteousness, the planting of the Lord, that He may be glorified.

What sticks out for me in this passage is 'those who mourn in Zion', which refers to those of us who are in the Church. It is not exclusive rather it is a beginning, for we the Church must show the way and by our love lead others to Christ. Also the following verse says:

Then they will rebuild the ancient ruins, they will raise up the former devastations; and they will repair the ruined cities, the desolations of many generations.

Those who are set free will go on to rebuild and repair in the Kingdom of God. Isn't that exciting? I am thrilled at what our God can do for sufferers of many things but certainly sufferers with mental health problems. There is light at the end of the tunnel!

One thing I will say, however, is healing cannot be manufactured and it is hard when it doesn't come. Laments are valid, as seen in the Psalms, Ezekiel and Lamentations alike; it was useful to write down my own lament while I was ill – it is like a description of where you are at, but directed to God and it doesn't have to have a happy ending. God is not ashamed of us, give it to Him. He does not mind, He knows about it already.

My heart goes out to all who are awaiting their release. My brother, my sister the road you travel seems uphill and rocky, but when you get to the top there are amazing views. Stop along the way and look, look to our great and wonderful God.

He is our Father; He formed us in the depths of the earth and numbers every hair on our head. He is with us in our suffering, He never leaves us. Jesus saved us and whatever we may think of ourselves, He died for us because we are worth it; He is interceding for us as for all of the saints and, yes, you are a saint! Call on Him, call on the Holy Spirit and be filled afresh. Let Him comfort you and give you hope, for there is always hope despite your worst thoughts, your worst fears, your worst anxieties and your painful existence. Remember that we have a high priest, our saviour, who can sympathise with our weaknesses and has been tempted in every way as we are, yet is without sin. 'Therefore let us draw near with confidence to the throne of grace, so that we may receive mercy and find grace to help in time of need.' (Hebrews 4:16)

16: What Friends and Family Can Do

I have heard many cries: 'but what can I do to help?'. Fortunately there are answers, though it will be by trial and error that we can learn how to help our loved ones with mental illness. Forging relationship with another human being mirrors the Trinity, where God the Father, Jesus the Son and the Holy Spirit are in perfect unity, perfect connection with one another, perfect relationship. Being real with one another forms connections. I quote from Larry Crabb's book *Connecting*:

> *When people make their struggles known, those who listen usually feel uncomfortable and uncertain of what to do. Most of us end up giving advice or reassurance... We rarely see such moments as opportunity for powerful connection, or, if we do, we're not sure how to seize it.*

With our mentally ill friend or family member, we must seize the opportunity, even if it's in our small way. If we think it's not good enough we are in a good place with the Father as He delights to be strong when we are weak. Here are some suggestions:

- Keep in touch. Even if this is hard and everything in you wants to turn away because of your own lack of confidence.
- Be approachable. Whether this is for a short chat or a longer conversation. It is vital not to give the sufferer the feeling that they are being rejected.

- Do send get well cards, presents or flowers as you would for anyone who is suffering from a physical complaint.

- Be led by the sufferer. When someone is very unwell, then a conversation might require a lot of effort by that person.

- If you can show physical affection, do so. Even the squeeze of a hand might speak eons to a person who thinks of himself or herself as rotten or worthless.

- Keep in contact even when you think you are suffering from rejection by the person concerned – it may just be their sick brain not functioning correctly.

- Do not expect the sick person to be 'fun' whether you are visiting them, taking them out or meeting for a social event. That way you will not be disappointed, but you may get a nice surprise if they are feeling better!

- Do cherish your family member or friend. Compassion and kindness are not easily forgotten.

- Do ask the sufferer how they think they are getting on. It's not good to rely on others' opinions.

- Do evaluate your visit or presence with the sufferer. You may feel you have been of no use at all, but the person concerned may have found it really helpful.

- Be honest about your own situation. Sharing life is good, but be sensitive not to weigh the sufferer down with too many of your worries or concerns.

- Do keep praying even if the situation seems hopeless or seems to be going on for a long time. Just keep presenting your friend or loved one to the Father until such a time as you hear from God that it's time to stop.

- Listen to God and hear what He is saying about the situation.

- If you have a prophecy or a 'word', weigh up carefully whether it is right to share it with the person or just to pray it into being. It may prove to be too much of a pressure if it is shared at an untimely moment.

- Do not bring judgement or condemning words. If God reveals sin in someone's life – PRAY for them. Please do not be a 'Job's comforter'.

- Suffer *with* another member of the body, not at a distance. The battle is to find God not to solve problems.

- Do not lose heart as God our heavenly Father, Jesus the Son and the Holy Spirit can do abundantly more than we can ask or think. Keep positive.

If you know a person who is suffering mental illness but also seems to be very 'demanding', the key thing is not to reject them. However it is perfectly alright to lay down boundaries. For instance, if they keep phoning you inappropriately, ask them to stop but at the same time say, 'but I will phone *you*' and give a specific day and/or time. If someone constantly wants attention to their wounds or areas of self harm, again you do not have to deal with it – it is perfectly appropriate to refer them to their practice nurse or if serious to A&E – there they will get the follow up support that they need.

There are help lines available in your locality; it may well be a good idea to familiarise yourself with these. If you are out of your depth, then ask for help from your church leader. If you want to get in touch with the sufferer's GP, it is better if the patient makes contact themselves, so ask them to do so, but if all else fails, then go ahead. However do not expect any feedback as the patient has absolute confidentiality with their GP and he/she may not be able to talk to you without the patient's consent. If you are worried that the person may be about to commit suicide or serious self harm, then phone 999 to call an ambulance or the police. They are trained to take the person to a place of safety where they will be assessed for their mental condition. If someone is behaving in a bizarre way that is out of character for them, it may also be appropriate to get them to their GP or the local A&E department. In the rare event of someone turning violent, then a 999 call should be made and the situation explained.

Finally remain close to God yourself and don't worry if you make mistakes. None of us are perfect and our heavenly Father delights in redeeming situations.

If you are worried about your own mental health, please get help. See your GP, see your church leader, see a counsellor, there is no shame in becoming vulnerable: 'That is why for Christ's sake, I delight in weaknesses, in insults, in hardships, in persecutions, in difficulties. For when I am weak, then I am strong.' (2 Corinthians 12: 10)

Let me finish with a quote from Hebrews 4:15–16, which gives us every reason to bring our lives to the Lord. He is a good God and, though we may not know why we suffer, He invites us near.

For we do not have a high priest who is unable to sympathise with our weaknesses, but we have one who has been tempted in every way, just as we are – yet was without sin. Let us then approach the throne of grace with confidence, so that we may receive mercy and find grace to help us in our time of need.

Books and Resources

Crabb, L. *Shattered Dreams* (Colorado Springs: Waterbrook Press, 2001)

Crabb, L. *Connecting* (Nashville: Thomas Nelson Inc, 2005)

Kendall, R.T. *Total Forgiveness* (London: Hodder & Stoughton, 2001)

Kendall, R.T. *Totally Forgiving Ourselves* (London: Hodder & Stoughton, 2007)

Lewis, C.S. *The Problem of Pain* (London: Harper Collins, 2002)

Olthuis, J. *The Beautiful Risk* (Grand Rapids: Zondervan, 2001)

Stibbe, M. *From Orphans to Heirs* (Abingdon: BRF, 2005)

Stibbe, M. *The Father You've Been Waiting For* (Milton Keynes: Authentic Media, 2005)

Useful UK Phone Numbers

UCB Prayer Line: 0845 456 7729
Samaritans: 08457 90 90 90
Premier Lifeline: 0845 345 0707 (BT Local Rate),
020 7316 0808